MARCO  POLO

Tips

LAKE GARDA

GERMANY
Stuttgart
Munich
F
Bern
AUSTRIA
SWITZERLAND
Bolzano
Lake Garda
SLOVENIA
Milan
Trieste
CROATIA
Verona
Venice
Genoa
ITALY
Adriatic
Sea
SAN MARINO
Ligurian
Sea
Florence

← INSIDE FRONT COVER:
THE BEST HIGHLIGHTS

The best Insider Tips → p. 4

INSIDER TIP

Best of ... → p. 7

North shore → p. 32

East shore → p. 50

4   THE BEST INSIDER TIPS

6   BEST OF ...
● GREAT PLACES FOR FREE p. 6
● ONLY ON LAKE GARDA p. 7
● AND IF IT RAINS? p. 8
● RELAX AND CHILL OUT p. 9

10   INTRODUCTION

16   WHAT'S HOT

18   IN A NUTSHELL

24   FOOD & DRINK

28   SHOPPING

30   THE PERFECT ROUTE

32   NORTH SHORE
LIMONE, MALCESINE, RIVA DEL GARDA,
TORBOLE

50   EAST SHORE
BARDOLONO, GARDA, LAZISE, TORRI DEL
BENACO

70   SOUTH SHORE
DESENZANO, SIRMIONE

SYMBOLS

INSIDER TIP   Insider Tip

★   Highlight

●●●●   Best of ...

↘↗   Scenic view

☺   Responsible travel: for eco-
logical or fair trade aspects

(*)   Telephone numbers that
are not toll-free

PRICE CATEGORIES
HOTELS

Expensive   over 120 euros

Moderate   80–120 euros

Budget   under 80 euros

Price for a double room,
including breakfast,
in the low season

PRICE CATEGORIES
RESTAURANTS

Expensive   over 35 euros

Moderate   25–35 euros

Budget   under 25 euros

Prices are for a meal with a
starter, main course and one
drink

On the cover: Panoramic cable-car ride up Monte Baldo p. 40 | A garden full of surprises p. 93

CONTENTS

WEST SHORE 80
GARDONE RIVIERA, GARGNANO, SALÒ

TRIPS & TOURS 96

SPORTS & ACTIVITIES 102

TRAVEL WITH KIDS 106

FESTIVALS & EVENTS 110

LINKS, BLOGS, APPS & MORE 112

TRAVEL TIPS 114

USEFUL PHRASES 120

ROAD ATLAS 126

INDEX & CREDITS 138

DOS & DON'TS 140

South shore → p. 70

West shore → p. 80

Trips & tours → p. 96

Road atlas → p. 126

DID YOU KNOW?
Timeline → p. 12
Local specialities → p. 26
Books & films → p. 88
Markets & market
days → p. 115
Weather → p. 117
Currency converter → p. 118
Budgeting → p. 119

MAPS IN THE GUIDEBOOK
(128 A1) Page numbers
and coordinates refer to
the road atlas
(0) Site/address located off
the map coordinates are also
given for places that are not
marked on the road atlas

Streets maps of Bardolino,
Riva del Garda, Salò and
Sirmione can be found inside
the back cover

**INSIDE BACK COVER:
PULL-OUT MAP →**

PULL-OUT MAP 🔲
(🔲 A1) Refers to the
removable pull-out map

The best MARCO POLO Insider Tips

Our top 15 Insider Tips

INSIDER TIP **Homemade ice cream**

There are two good reasons for stopping for an ice cream in the *Gelateria Cento per Cento:* to build up your reserves before climbing up to Malcesine castle and as a reward for having got down again. Fabrizio Bottesi's ice cream is so good that even locals beat a path up the steep road to it → p. 37

INSIDER TIP **Cheese and wine**

Hella, the proprietor at the *Osteria Santo Cielo* in Malcesine, is Dutch and was tempted to settle in the area by the delicious food and wine. Guests can enjoy a platter of different cheeses or locally produced salami in her *osteria* washed down with local wines served in large goblets → p. 39

INSIDER TIP **Hiking with a difference**

The 4 km-long (2½ mi) path from Torbole to Tempesta is quite an adventure. You'll find yourself walking up and down seemingly never-ending metal steps along the rock face. A panoramic path with information boards → p. 48

INSIDER TIP **'Gorge'-ous green**

Lago di Valvestino, actually created by building a dam across a stream, is a vibrant green paradise hidden in a nature reserve → p. 89

INSIDER TIP **All-in-one shop**

Concept store, art gallery, designer shop and winebar: La Barchessa Arte in the historical Palazzo Rambaldi in Bardolino is all four rolled into one (photo above) → p. 53

INSIDER TIP **Free climbing without vertigo**

The best of the best take part in the inofficial Rock Master competition for free climbers in Arco. Spectators can watch this nerve-racking sport from a safe distance (photo right) → p. 103

INSIDER TIP **Hidden delights**

Sans Souci is a small *osteria* in a vaulted cellar. This is where the locals from Gardone meet. After all, they don't need a view of the lake – they have that at home → p. 84

INSIDER TIP Treetop walk

A thrill for children and adults alike: you scramble among the treetops in the Jungle Adventure Park near San Zeno di Montagna → **p. 109**

INSIDER TIP Relaxed cycling tours without map-reading problems

Cycling in the hilly area around Desenzano is pure bliss. You can pick up a brochure with GPS routes for cyclists from the tourist information office → **p. 74**

INSIDER TIP Church with a view

The view from the church square in Albisano of the lake is stunning. Why this is called the 'balcony of Lake Garda' is pretty obvious! → **p. 69**

INSIDER TIP Outward bound

If you find the beach too boring, then book a tour with Skyclimber in Tremosine for a fixed-rope climb, a canyoning trip or something similar. Intended for 'normal' people who like having a good time rather than just for the extreme athletic → **p. 90**

INSIDER TIP Head in the clouds

Baita dei Forti is just a stone's throw from the cable-car station at the top of Monte Baldo where you can tuck into good wholesome fare. An added extra: you can even stay the night here and the fabulous views of the lake are free → **p. 41**

INSIDER TIP Museum with that *déjà vu* feeling

The Archeological Museum in Sirmione's Grotte di Catullo presents ancient history in a modern way → **p. 76**

INSIDER TIP Ceramic art

No two of Mariano Fuga's delicate porcelain figures are alike. These individual pieces make pretty souvenirs and can be found in his studio in Gargnano → **p. 88**

INSIDER TIP Rustic refuge

Antica Cascina Liano, with its heavy wooden ceiling is located in a rural corner in the parish of Gargnano and is a cosy place to stay → **p. 87**

BEST OF ...

FOR FREE

● *Rock engravings*
Most walks are free of charge but this one that starts in Garda comes with something different: rock engravings that point to the early settlement of this region. The route is well waymarked. You'll find the engravings in the wooded area not far from Punta San Vigilio → p. 59

● *Jogging circuit*
In summer you'll have to rise early if you want to work up a sweat without being in the scorching sun. But you'll enjoy this relaxing five-km (3-mi) route along the pedestrianised promenade around the bay of Salò → p. 93

● *Sunsets*
It may not be Capri and the sun doesn't set into the sea, but it's a pretty sight watching the sun go down from the lakeside on the harbour wall in Desenzano, for example. Naturally theatrical → p. 70

● *Jazz for free*
A number of events as part of the Gardajazz event are held in the northern most corner of the lake during the summer. The 'Jazz-Café' concerts are all free of charge → p. 38

● *Beautiful beach*
The Lido delle Bionde in Sirmione is one of the loveliest beaches on Lake Garda – and there isn't even an entrance fee. Consisting of only a narrow strip of pebbles it is located below the archeological sites. The long wooden jetty is particularly pretty, even without the blondes *(bionde)*! (photo) → p. 78

● *Church concert*
The acoustics are particularly good: classical concerts are held on Mondays in summer in San Severo Church in Bardolino. Listening to music in the Romanesque building is a delightful experience → p. 52

○●●● Dots in guidebook refer to 'Best of ...' tips

● *Scaliger Castle*

The powerful Scaliger family of Verona ruled over the east shore for centuries. In the 13th and 14th centuries they built two castles as a sign of their strength: in Malcesine, in Torri del Benaco and in Sirmione. Find out for yourself which is the most beautiful! → p. 37, 67 and 77

● *Fish from the lake*

Some 50 professional fishermen on the lake catch what both visitors and locals like to eat: whitefish, trout and the rare Lake Garda trout called *carpione*. The day's catch is sold at the fish cooperative market in Garda → p. 59

● *A glass of Bardolino*

The vineyards that produce the Bardolino wine are on the slopes above the village of the same name. You can sample and buy wine directly from the producers along the Strada del Vino → p. 56

● *Boat trips*

Just how beautifully the villages snuggle into the hills along the lakeside can best be seen from the water. And whoever wants to explore the opposite side of the lake can simply take a ferry between Torri and Toscolano. But taking the boat is also a good idea when simply visiting the market in the next village along the shore (photo) → p. 117

● *Mountain paradise for the very active*

Many outdoor enthusiasts can be found on Monte Baldo – either racing downhill on bikes (which can be hired near the cable-car at the bottom of the mountain), paragliding in tandem, hiking to the summit or skiing down the slopes in winter → p. 96, 102 and 103

● *Catullus Caves*

Whether the Latin poet Gaius Valerius Catullus, from the 1st century BC, lived near the site of this imposing villa is questionable. But a visit ot the archeological digs in Sirmione is worthwhile at any rate → p. 76

● *Spectacular mountain bike route*

The Sentiero del Ponale di Giacomo Cis near Riva, with a difference in altitude of 850 m (2625 ft), is one of the best-known routes on Lake Garda and, consequently, you'll never be on your own. First fight your way to the top, then speed back down again → p. 115

ONLY IN

BEST OF ...

● **Salò Cathedral**
The late Gothic cathedral of Santa Maria Annunziata in Salò is the largest church on the lake. And it boasts a strange and fascinating curiosity: walk back and forth over the mosaic in the floor and you'll be amazed at the three-dimensional effect it has – even without 3-D glasses! → p. 92

● **City trip**
There are three ways to keep out of the rain on a visit to nearby Verona: visit one of its many museums, its famous churches such as San Zeno, and all sorts of inviting shops. You can drift from one boutique to the next along the Via Mazzini → p. 65

● **Classique**
This restaurant is located in an historical villa on the lakeside prom-enade in Lazise. From its high vantage point you can look out across the windswept lake – especially suitable for getting warm again after a walk in the rain → p. 62

● **Varone waterfall**
It makes no real difference what the weather is doing: the waterfall created by the Tenno stream sends a veil of spray into this narrow gorge (photo). 'A hellish spectacle' noted Thomas Mann → p. 45

● **Pasticceria Vassalli**
Try the exquisite noisette chocolates, *bacetti di Salò* ('kisses from Salò'), in this time-honoured café in Salò to accompany your cappuccino or hot chocolate. And, at long last, you'll have time to write your postcards! → p. 92

● **Lakeside walk**
Don't be put off by the weather! When the rain whips up waves on the otherwise so calm lake, the beaches and promenades are empty. In Torbole you'll be able to watch the intrepid (kite)surfers who, of course, are out there in all weathers → p. 105

RAIN

CHILL OUT

● *Gardacqua*
If the lake isn't enough then you can have all the water you want in this mixture between a large open-air swimming pool, spa complex and exclusive leisure centre in Garda → **p. 59**

● *Yoga*
Relaxing on a yoga mat: you can choose between several yoga courses in Riva – unwind on the lakeside (photo) → **p. 44**

● *My meadow*
When was the last time you lay down in a grassy field and simply stared into the sky, watched the clouds scud past while listening to the leaves rustling in the olive trees or the birds singing? You could do this for example on the Via Santa Lucia from Torbole to Nago → **p. 47**

● *Parco Termale del Garda*
This spa complex with underwater massage jets and fountains is also open in winter → **p. 64**

● *Giardino Heller*
Of all the many parks on the west shore, the Old Botanic Garden in Gardone, that was taken over by the all-round artist André Heller, is certainly one of the most unusual. Sitting on benches beneath ancient trees, you can take in the Tibetan prayer flags, modern art and water fountains while listening to the birds → **p. 82**

● *Open-air concerts*
Concerts are frequently held outside in summer. The sound of an orchestra performing on a balmy evening – an idyllic holiday memory → **p. 110 and 111**

● *Hot springs in Sirmione*
Even the Romans knew how to make the most of Sirmione's hot springs. Aquaria, of more recent construction comprises a large pool landscape with extensive spa facilities and a beauty section → **p. 79**

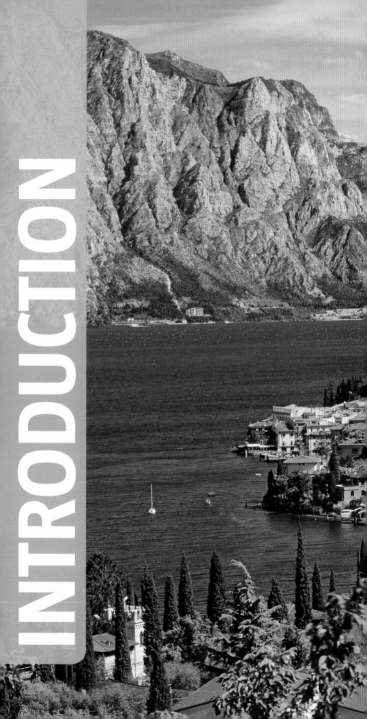

INTRODUCTION

DISCOVER LAKE GARDA!

There are not very many lakes that have so many varied facets and can satisfy so many different people's idea of the perfect holiday. For those of you seeking peace and quiet who don't like to hear anything when you're reading a book or newspaper but the gentle flapping of sails in the wind and the sound of moored boats rubbing shoulders, then Gargnano is the place for you. Peace reigns supreme half way down the west shore. Classy hotels are traditional on this part of the lake. In the late 19th century, German hotelier Louis Wimmer recognised the charm of Lake Garda and built the first grand hotel, in Gardone. Others soon followed. A rather old-fashioned, respectable tourism still prevails there.

If you're gregarious and want people around you till late, Bardolino and Garda will suit you. The little lanes of the Old Towns are almost more crowded in the evenings than during the day, and you still see little children running around with ice creams in their hands at midnight. Young adults will head for the south shore if a real nightlife is what they've come for. Some of the biggest discos in Italy are in and around Desenzano.

Photo: Malcesine on the northeast shore

Country fare from the Trento district is served I La Montanara in a lane in Riva's Old Town

If a sporting holiday is your thing, go north. The north shore sometimes seems to be one large adventure playground. In the steep valleys and wild streams of Trentino there's a tradition of kayaking, swimming, windsurfing and sailing. The latest sport to have been added is rafting. If all that is not enough, you can even try canyoning. Enveloped in neoprene suits and equipped with helmets and lifejackets, adventure sports fans plunge into ravines – under professional guidance, one trusts. There's even a season for diving on the lake. With luck – or a guide – you can locate sunken galleys from the period of Venetian rule.

Mountain bikers and hikers roam the mountain slopes. Where it gets steep, rock climbers ascend vertical rockfaces, sometimes directly over the lake. On summer weekends, tourist offices of the 'Olive Riviera' organise excursions and guided tours to Monte

After 2000 BC
Celts, Raetians and Venetians settle in the Lake Garda area

15 BC
The Romans arrive at the lake and name it 'Benacus'

9th/10th centuries
Carolingian emperors and kings, as well as local princes, fight for supremacy in Upper Italy

1260–1387
The Scaligers rule in and around Verona

1387–1405
The Milanese Visconti family rules over the Lake Garda area

Baldo. There are botanical excursions, tours to church festivals and moonlight hikes. And on the lake, the armada of surfers carry on their battles with or against the wind – from the shore, it's not always so easy to distinguish which. The steep mountains have a funnel effect, regularly creating quite strong winds.

The fact that Lake Garda offers such diverse outdoor activities has a further advantage. In the evening you can tuck into mountains of pasta since you've spent all day burning off those calories. That's just as well because the food here is excellent (as long as you avoid the excessively touristy places, often those directly by the harbours), whether it's a lavish three-course meal in a gourmet restaurant in Salò or a simple Lake Garda grilled trout. Even though the hordes of tourists show no signs of abating, the food is getting better. They say that more and more cooks are returning to their roots – to mama's home cooking. But it is also a fact that demand has changed, and with it the food. More and more holidaymakers want the real thing – traditional Lake Garda dishes and fresh ingredients.

The same applies to wine. Whereas 20 years ago, holidaymakers still used to buy large bottles in straw holders, the demand is now for quality. The Strada del Vino in the hills behind Bardolino is very popular

> **Peace all around in the middle of the west shore**

for that very reason. While Italian red wine has become increasingly full bodied, winegrowers and lovers have rediscovered the rosé. Slightly chilled Bardolino *chiaretto*, the Lake Garda rosé, is the perfect match for a light summer meal.

1405–1797 The Venetians take control of the east shore

1797 The west shore is taken over by Napoleon's Cisalpine Republic; Austria is given the east shore and Verona

1814/15 After Napoleon's overthrow, the Congress of Vienna grants Austria Lombardy and the Veneto

1821–1861 Risorgimento period, the movement for Italian unification. Italy becomes a sovereign state in 1861

1919 After World War I, the Lake is now completely Italian

In Malcesine you can hike in the mountains in the morning and lie on the beach in the afternoon

On the other shore, heading north from Gargnano, you can still see how people made a living on Lake Garda before the tourists came. *Limonaie* are where lemons were grown. Generally, the meagre income from agriculture or fishing was not enough to keep a family. In the 19th century, many inhabitants of Lake Garda's villages emigrated to try their luck in America. Before the arrival of tourism, Lake Garda was a poor region where life was simple and hard. In the chestnut and pine forests above Gargnano people carried on the archaic business of charcoal-burning, while the women worked the narrow strips of land from early morning till late at night.

> **Many chefs are finding out more about their roots**

1943–45
Republic of Salò: the Fascist dictator Mussolini withdraws to the lake towards the end of World War II

1946
After a referendum, Italy becomes a republic and the king goes into exile in Portugal

1962
The cable car from Malcesine to the top of Monte Baldo is opened

2001
A new tunnel is constructed between Riva and Limone

2006
The Gardaland Theatre is opened in the Gardaland leisure park

Artists and writers, but especially the latter, have always been attracted to Lake Garda. In 1786 Goethe enthused about the 'wonderful effect' of the lake during his trip to Italy. Around the turn of the 20th century, the Habsburg-ruled town of Riva attracted many illustrious guests, including Friedrich Nietzsche and Thomas Mann. In 1917, Franz Kafka also paid a visit.

Perhaps these early celebrities were, like modern visitors, on the look-out for cultural treasures. The Romanesque churches of Bardolino, San Zeno and San Severo are veritable gems, and Sant'Andrea in Maderno is no less interesting. Other sights are found on short trips to places like Trento with its delightful Piazza Duomo or the Roman Arena in Verona. But you don't need to home in on cultural treasures and sights to enjoy the atmosphere of Lake Garda's towns and villages. The traditional buildings in their centres are astonishingly well preserved as a stroll along the narrow lanes and alleyways of the Old Towns will show you.

Life on the lake is nowadays largely governed by tourism. It is of course not just those directly affected by the streams of tourists (hoteliers and restaurateurs, for example) who make a living from them. Fruit vendors selling at market stalls, craftsmen rebuilding holiday homes, Lake Garda fishermen supplying the *trattorias*, cheese-producing dairy farmers up in the mountains and even solitary truffle-hunters are also dependent on them.

While tourism is a blessing for the region on the one hand, it is also a curse. The heavy traffic in particular is a problem. It therefore makes sense not to use the car too much when holidaying on the lake. And, to be quite honest, it's also more fun without! By taking the boat to the market in the next village and feeling the wind on your face will save you a nerve-racking hunt for somewhere to park and the parking fee. By using the buses which run frequently and on time to visit a village you can enjoy a glass of wine while there

The old villages and towns are surprisingly well looked after

without worrying. And if you go off on a hike you don't have to return to where you started but can simply take a bus. An even more appealing alternative is cycling. On the East Shore in particular the cycle path along the lake is continuously being improved and extended and you can hire bicycles at many hotels. You don't even need to be sporty at all to pedal along the lakeside or to a beach. But if you really want to earn that dish of pasta properly, just zoom up and down a couple of hills through the vineyards.

Yet despite the strong concentration on tourism, you don't need to worry about being ripped off as a holidaymaker. Requests for bus timetables, or information about bathing and biking centres, are treated very civilly in tourist offices. In many hotels, you are welcomed as if you have been a regular visitor for years and in the restaurant in the evening the waiter may well casually burst into song. Lake Garda values its visitors – and vice versa.

WHAT'S HOT

1 Green vineyards

Organic-issimo Young wine-growers go green. The *Cantina della Valtenesi e della Lugana (Via Pergola 21, Moniga del Garda, www.civielle.com)* produces wines with romantic names such as Biocora – 'the dance of life'. There is also an organic Bardolino, including the prize-winning *Cantina di Custoza (Strada Staffalo 1, Custoza, www.cantinadicustoza.it)*. *Gardenali (Via XXV Aprile 8, Volta Mantovana, www.gardenali.it)* does not just cultivate grapes but other organic fruit as well, in keeping with the current overall trend.

Wind and snow

2

Snow-kiting A vibrant winter sport's scene is emerging on Lake Garda. Kiters who race across the water in summer switch to snowboards in the winter, strap on their inflatable kites or gliders and take over Monte Baldo. This is possible thanks to the unusual thermals found during the winter months. *Waterproof (Via Lavesino 9, Brenzone sul Garda, www.waterproof.net)* can teach both beginners and experienced kiters new tricks. The powder snow on the slopes is just as appealing to other winter sports enthusiasts on conventional snowboards available from the *Scuola Sci Malcesine (Tratto Spino, scuolasci malcesine.bloog.it)*.

3 De luxe camping

Luxurious 'glamping' – glamour camping – is trendy. *Selectcamp (www.selectcamp.co.uk)* is a specialist in this field and can accommodate happy campers in luxury bungalow tents, for example in *Camping Bella Italia (Via Bella Italia 2, Peschiera del Garda, photo)*, where you can relax on a private beach with direct access to the water. In *Camping Fontanelle (Via*

There are a lot of things to discover on Lake Garda. Here is our hand-picked selection

Magone 13, Moniga del Garda) and *Camping Weekend (Via Vallone della Selva 2, San Felice del Benaco)* each tent has its own terrace.

Canyoning

4

Nervenkitzel im Felsen Palvicio, Vajo dell' Orsa and Splish Splash are known throughout the world in the canyoning scene. All three gorges can be navigated on organised three-day tours to test your nerves. The *Canyoning Center Gardasee (Trattoria Ca' Orsa, Affi, www.outdoorplanet.net, photo)* offers ten different tours of varying degrees of difficulty – fun for all the family and a thrilling adventure. The *Canyoning Center Wet Way (Garda Avventura, Via Sant'Andrea 16 e, Arco, www.wetway.net)* explores the gorges around Lake Garda from the end of April until mid October.

Festivals with a difference

5

It's the fun-factor that really counts! The odder the festival the more popular it is, and lovers of the unconventional are well rewarded on Lake Garda. In autumn, bloggers descend on Riva del Garda and celebrate the *Blog Festival (www.blogfest.it, photo)* in the historical Old Town. Events range from debates to concerts and from award ceremonies to games. The *Tortellini Festival (Festa del nodo d'amore, book under www.valeggio.com)* in Valeggio sul Mincio is to honour the noodle. Once a year the medieval Visconti Bridge is turned into an open-air restaurant. Hungry pasta lovers can look forward to more than 600,000 handmade tortellini. The *Drodesera Fies Festival (Centrale Fies, Dro, www.centralefies.it)* focuses on contemporary art. Every summer art performances are held in a hydro-electric power station that is still in everyday use.

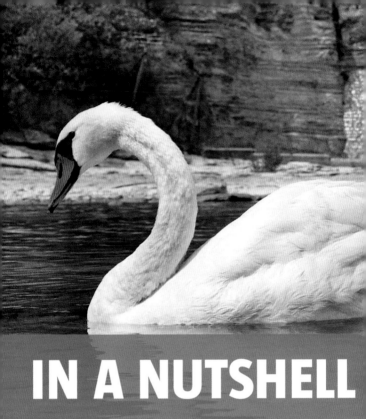

IN A NUTSHELL

BLUE FLAG

Time and again the names of beaches on Lake Garda that had received the Blue Flag award *(www.blueflag.org)* were proudly announced. More recently, only Sirmione was given this award for particularly clean water and other criteria that help promote sustainable tourism, such as separate litter bins for different waste products and accessibility by public transport. Awards are made by the FEE (Foundation for Environmental Education), a non-profit organisation for the protection of the environment. In the past few years, however, even Sirmione was no longer awarded the *Bandiera Blu* – which now means that there are no Blue Flags on Lake Garda. To improve the quality of the water in European lakes, the EU project 'Eulakes' was launched which also includes Lake Garda. Eulakes aims at restricting lakeside development, protecting the quality of the water and researching into climatic changes.

EXCAVATIONS

The Romans called Lake Garda 'Benacus' and traces of settlements are frequently found during building work today. The most famous remains are the Grotte di Catullo in Sirmione. In Desenzano, a beautiful floor mosaic can still be marvelled at and, near Riva, the Romans also built a place of worship.

Photo: Swans on the south shore

A paradise for botanists and birds:
on wildlife, islands and delicious truffles
as well as languages and history

Only recently, construction workers came across traces of a Roman villa – probably from the 5th century AD – in Castelletto cemetery. It is one of the most important finds of its kind in the Lake Garda/Verona area, even in the whole Veneto region.

FAUNA

Water fowl don't particularly like the lake, since there is little cover on the shore for them to hide and breed, but there are all sorts of gulls and ducks flying around – and more are more swans are to be seen. However, numerous migratory species pass this way, producing an interesting mixture of North African and northern European species. A pair of golden eagles have taken up residence in the Parco Alto Garda, and capercaillies have also been seen there. You'll have to be a real expert to be able to distinguish between the 959 varieties of butterfly that have been identified around the lake. Even if you don't know their names, they are still pretty to look at waving gently in the breeze on lavender bushes. Native species such as fire salamanders and green lizards can frequently be seen on walls. The poisonous asp viper and adders also occur occasionally, so stout shoes are recommended! Even lynxes have returned to Lake Garda, with sightings of this shy wild animal being reported in the upper mountain regions of the Parco Alto Garda.

Dense vegetation on the west shore: Giardino Hruska in Gardone

FLORA

Cultivated plants dominate the image of the lake. On the northwest shore are the already-mentioned lemon groves, now regrettably abandoned, while in the east and south gentle vineyards alternate with olive groves. Monte Baldo which is also known as the 'Garden of Europe' is an eldorado for botanists. As its crest loomed out over the glaciers in the Ice Age, plants have managed to survive that are not known anywhere else, like the endemic Mt Baldo wind rose (Anemone baldensis). Somewhat lower down, cyclamens grow wild in the shade of large holm oaks and beeches. At home in the Parco Alto Garda, on the high plateau of Tremosine, is the sole insect-eating species in the area, the alpine butterwort (Pinguicula alpina). Rare fire lilies (Lilium bulbiferum) and lady's slipper orchids grow here. Along the shore itself, you'll find yourself among dense Mediterranean vegetation. In Maderno, oleander trees line the shore, mimosa and camellias grow in the park-like gardens of Gardone Riviera, magnolias provide shade along the Desenzano shore road and you can sit under palm trees on the lovely promenade in Salò. All round the lake, roses proliferate on espaliers on house walls, their heads nodding to passers-by.

GARDESANA

Expletives can be heard from many a car driver: 30 km/h (20 mph) speed restrictions along the stretch of road from Riva del Garda to Gargnano and 74 tunnels. Some are so narrow that two motorhomes can only just pass and if there is a group of cyclists then ... The 'Gardesana Occidentale', however, is considered one of the most beautiful roads in Italy. And wherever openings in tunnels and galleries reveal glimpses of the lake, then you'll realise why. It was built after World War I, not for tourists, but to link the north of the lake – which at that time became part of Italy – to the south. The slightly wider and not quite so spectacular 'Gardesana Orientale' runs along the opposite bank. As the old roads can-

near Salò. For a few years now it has been possible to visit it (for further information please refer to the descriptions of Garda and Salò). Just 2 km (1¼ mi) further south, in Manerba and San Felice bay, is *Isola San Biagio* and its neighbour *I Conigli*

Spectacularly built along and through the rock face: the Gardesana Occidentale

not cope with today's amount of traffic at all, both routes are closed to lorries in the summer.

SLANDS

Although Lake Garda cannot boast such famous islands as Lago Maggiore or Lake Orta, it does have a few small isles. The largest, Isola del Garda *(www.isoladel garda.com)* with the Villa Borghese, is

(rabbit island). San Biagio is a popular place for a day out – and when the water is low you can walk across to it from the mainland with your swimming things under your arm. *Isola Trimelone* lies off Assenza between Porto di Brenzone and Malcesine; it is a military zone and cannot be visited – until now at any rate. The island was used for storing munition and more than 5000 bombs of various sizes have so far been removed. Since the island has been out-of-bounds for so long, it has become an oasis for migrating birds. It is still uncertain if it will be made accessible to tourists after all the bombs have gone.

LANGUAGES AND NATIONALITIES

The English love the section between Salò and Riva and, even without a word of Italian, English-speaking holidaymakers manage very well on Lake Garda and will certainly end up with the supper they want. The area really can't complain about a lack of tourists who come from all over Europe. You can't really not hear the Germans who, at almost 60 percent, account for the largest ex-pat group and 40 percent of the area's annual visitors. They tend to stick to the north and east shores from Riva down to Peschiera. The Dutch love both the west and east shore while the Italians tend to head for the area around Gardone and Salò. German and Dutch visitors don't necessarily need to try hard at speaking Italian either, as many waiters can speak these languages as well – not to mention the many seasonal workers on the lake: there are British DJs, Bavarian surfing instructors and Dutch girls behind the bar. Yet the local dialect from the Lake Garda area is still popular with the young locals – perhaps it's the only language to be at home in when the streets and squares are full of the babble of foreign languages.

LEISURE PARKS

Italians love them – huge holiday parks such as you find around Peschiera. But more recently they have come in for criticism, especially after the death of two dolphins in Gardaland. The management ascribed the deaths to natural causes, but a trainer accused them of subjecting the animals to excessive stress. That has not diminished the appeal of large theme parks in Italy one iota – Gardaland and other similar places have been providing entertainment for years, with more than 3 million people visiting Gardaland alone every year.

MONTE BALDO TRUFFLE

The truffle (or *tartufo* in Italian) is a fungus – but what a misnomer for such an exquisite culinary delight! They grow underground among the roots of deciduous trees and can also be found on Monte Baldo. A 'truffle week' is held in San Zeno di Montagna every October and during this time truffles can be sampled in several local restaurants. Truffles also occur on the west shore of the lake around Tignale. Pigs were traditionally used to snuffle out truffles which they reliably found – but were only too eager to gobble up themselves. Nowadays dogs are used instead. Hunting for truffles in restricted by law: only official *tartufari* are allowed to dig for the expensive tubers. Private individuals looking for truffles can be fined for poaching! When buying truffles make sure they are firm and not worm-eaten. Wrapped up in a damp dishcloth, fresh truffles keep up to three days at the most in a fridge. It is best to use them straight away – and that's even possible on the simplest of camping gas stoves. Just fry up some eggs or scramble them and grate thin slices of truffle over them – or do the same with pasta or risotto.

There are more than 100 different types of truffle. The black Perigord truffle *(tuber melanosporum vitt)* is the one most frequently found on Lake Garda. The particularly valued white truffle however can also be found. October to January is the season for the latter, November to March for the black variety. The summer truffle

Fun is the name of the game in the leisure park: shark in Sealife Aquarium Gardaland

tartufo d'estate does not have such a strong aroma but is consequently considerably less expensive.

PEACE TRAIL

For many years the area round Lake Garda was time and again the scene of bitter conflicts and not only during the period the Scaliger dynasty. During World War I, the front between Italy and Austria ran through Trentino. The line is today the course of the 350 km-long (220-mi) Peace Trail *(Sentiero della Pace)*, waymarked by a white dove emblem. Walking the whole trail takes about 30 days. The route takes you from the Adamello area towards Riva del Garda, then from Monte Altissimo near Nago to Mori and down to Rovereto. No mountain hiking experience is needed for this stretch and the southern section between Riva, Rovereto and Folgaria is gentle walking too. There are reminders of the various wars to be found everywhere such as trenches and paths blasted into the sides of cliffs. You may even come across spent cartridges and rusty cutlery. The scenery along the long-distance path is often spectacular but, if you keep your eyes open, you will frequently be reminded about the frightful history that was played out along this route. The numbers of soldiers killed on both sides between 1915 and 1918 during the war fought out in the mountains is estimated at 150,000 to 180,000. Some two thirds died as a result of avalanches, landslides or the cold. From 10–13 December 1916 alone, more than 10,000 people perished. *www.enrosadira.it/sentierodellapace/ pace3.htm*

FOOD & DRINK

You'll certainly get your fair share of pizza round Lake Garda, but if you think it is a typical Italian dish you're wrong. There is no typical Italian cuisine as such. Food in Italy is a regional thing, and that applies equally to Lake Garda.

Assuming of course that you don't always order pizza and Viennese schnitzel (though there's absolutely nothing wrong in that – even Italians are fond of a slice of veal cooked in breadcrumbs, and do it well, under the name *cotoletta milanese*). Lake Garda cuisine is rather different. It draws on three neighbouring regions – Trentino in the north, the Veneto on the east shore and Lombardy in the west. If you dine in good restaurants, you can sample the differences between the three cuisines. What they share is featuring fish on the menu, so it's available all round the lake.

If you discover *sardine di lago* on the menu you shouldn't miss this opportunity. This is really something quite rare – after all, sardines are normally found in the sea. But there is one sub-species of the herring family *(Alosa fallax)* that lives in Lake Garda, called the twaite shad in English. These sardines only swim upstream in fresh water to spawn, just like salmon, but somewhere along the line they seem to have decided to stay in the lake. In olden days sardines were salted to preserve them. Before eating them,

Specialities from three regions: red wines are served with hearty dishes from the Alps and delicate white wines with fish from the lake

the salt was then washed off, they were cut into small pieces and mixed with pasta. *Spaghetti con sardine di lago* is still a much-loved delicacy today.

Trentino offers the most substantial cuisine since it is an Alpine region. Many dishes are thus almost too heavy for summer evenings by the lake. Who can summon up an appetite for ham or cheese dumplings in a heat wave? They are just a reminder that maybe one should try visiting Lake Garda in winter some time. Everything is quieter then, and if you're shivering outside in a cold wind, hot filling food is just the thing. Another benefit of a winter stay is that December is the truffle *(tartufo)* picking season on the slopes of Monte Baldo. Truffles are a natural delicacy.

There's every variety of pasta, of course, for example tagliatelle with (mainly chanterelle) mushrooms *(tajadele co' i fonghi)*. The rice may come from the Po plain

LOCAL SPECIALITIES

PIATTI (DISHES)

▶ **alborelle** – fried lake fish
▶ **canederli** – dumplings; mostly eaten in the north
▶ **carne salada** – cured meat; Trentino's number one speciality
▶ **carpione** – the Lake Garda trout has become rare
▶ **coniglio** – rabbit; not only popular roasted; finely chopped rabbit is also served as a pasta ragout
▶ **funghi sott'olio** – (wild) mushrooms in oil, a typical ingredient of an *antipasto misto* – a mixed dish of starters
▶ **gnocchi** – small potato dumplings; a *primo* like pasta or a separate main course (photo left)
▶ **lavarello** – whitefish; if you are lucky, straight from the lake
▶ **prosciutto con melone** – (Parma) ham with honeydew melon, an *antipasti* classic
▶ **strangolapreti** – small spinach and bread dumplings taste best tossed in butter with crispy sage leaves
▶ **trota** – trout from the rivers and streams in the region (photo right)

BEVANDE (DRINKS)

▶ **Bardolino** – red wine from the east shore, a light wine, clear red in colour
▶ **birra alla spina** – draught beer; in Italy wine is rarely drunk with a pizza – beer is preferred
▶ **Lugana** – white wine from the south shore goes well with fish and pasta
▶ **Marzemino** – Trentino red wine, heavy, ruby red, velvety
▶ **Teroldego** – Trentino red wine, heavy, fruity, full-bodied

much further south, but nonetheless risottos are popular at the north end, usually made with boletus mushrooms (*porcini*). An indispensable side dish is polenta, a very filling paste made with maize flour, that is served throughout northern Italy. Hearty dishes like these call for equally strong wines. Two excellent reds made only in Trentino are Teroldego and Marzemino.

On the east shore, the typical wine is red Bardolino that meanwhile is of good quality. If you want to learn more about it, drive down the Strada del Vino. Fine white wines such as the Lugana in particular are found in the south east.

Less wine is produced on the west shore. If sparkling wine is what you like, keep an eye out for those from Franciacorta in the south west, made using the *méthode champenoise*.

Classic dishes of the south shore include courgette flowers stuffed with goats' cheese or the regional *bigoli* pasta variation. In the west, poultry is more common, e.g. breast of guinea fowl *(petto di faraona)*. A popular first course *(primo)* is *tortelli di zucca*, pasta envelopes with a pumpkin filling.

Neither Genoa nor Venice are far away, so Mediterranean dishes dominate the menus. Vegetables abound, either grilled as side dishes or pickled as a starter. Tomatoes feature everywhere. Once you've had them here in a *caprese* salad (tomatoes with mozzarella and fresh basil) or in a pasta sauce, you'll be less tolerant of those found on supermarket shelves in other countries.

With the desserts, it's the calories that matter. If a low count is what you want, order a *macedonia* of fresh fruit, or just ask for *frutta fresca* (fresh fruit). You'll get delicious apricots and peaches, nectarines or plums of a sweetness such as is rare at home.

And should you have eaten too much then try one of the many *grappas*, for which Trentino is famous. This fragrant, grape-based pomace liquor is normally drunk 'neat', sometimes served with pine needles, rowan berries or gentian root. The excellent *vino santo* from the area around Lake Toblino is less well known, made from *nosiola* grapes dried on wooden slats. This dessert wine was much favoured by members of the Council of Trent and, a report on a 'magnificent banquet' held on 25 July, 1546 by the Cardinal of Trento in a chrnonicle at the time tells of exquisite wines from the hills around Trento and 'vini dolci di Santa Massenza'.

As far as types of restaurant are concerned, round the lake you'll find more or less everything, from pizza takeaways to temples of haute cuisine (especially around Salò and Gargnano). During the high season, especially in more expensive restaurants, one thing is particularly important – make a reservation!

A note about the pizzerias: unfortunately, prices for the pre-eminent fast food have

Oenologically speaking the east shore is dominated by the Bardolino wine

risen dramatically, and you can now pay 8 euros or more, which is disproportionate to the cost of the ingredients. Often you can pay just a little bit more for more substantial, freshly prepared pasta or even a meat or fish dish in a better restaurant.

The weekly markets and food shops are to be recommended to those who don't want to splash out so much. For the price of two pizzas you can stock up on bread rolls, local cheese, salami, olives and of course tomatoes and perhaps a little basil and head for one of the beaches, a jetty or a slope overlooking the lake – *buon appetito!*

SHOPPING

Taking tasteful souvenirs back home from your stay in Italy is a way of prolonging the enjoyment. No problem. Almost every town round the lake has a weekly market. Whether it's smart shoes you want or top-quality Parmesan, chic handbags or stylish espresso machines, you'll find them here.

Opening times of shops vary enormously and are generally quite flexible as one would tend to expect in Italy. A rule of thumb is 9am until 12.30pm and 3.30pm until 7pm. In summer, shops are open till 10pm in many places, or sometimes even later. And in the busiest tourist resorts visitors can even part with their cash on Sundays.

CURTAINS

We're talking here of white *broderie anglaise* window curtains, a cross between a screen and insulation that can give every room an Italian touch. In Italy you find them everywhere. They are popular because they keep the summer heat out of the house without darkening interiors like closed shutters.

If you want to stock up on these for home, go to one of the larger markets, for example in Salò or Desenzano, or shops in larger towns round the lake. Mostly the shops are unspectacular, selling bed linens, cushion covers and the like, and are not aimed at tourists at all.

FASHION

Leather goods are still reasonably priced in Italy, especially at markets. Italian designer fashion is available in the brand boutiques of Salò and Peschiera, Desenzano, Riva and Bardolino. Sirmione is almost like one big shopping mall: the lanes in the Old Town are full of expensive shops waiting for tourists to come through the door flapping their credit cards.

Meantime, the hunt for inexpensive clothes can sometimes take odd forms. For example, numerous places have one-price shops, e.g. everything for 15 euros *(tutto a 15 euro)*, but often the goods offered are of such poor quality they do not even justify that price. On the increase is the number of 'outlets'. There will soon be one in every pedestrian precinct, but genuinely reduced designer clothes are

Pasta, shoes, sports gear: the weekly markets attract both locals and tourists alike

rare. Mostly they're full of cheap junk. However, you do find bargains if you're there in late summer. In end-of-season sales *(saldi)*, many shops discount all goods by 50 percent. The saving is particularly worthwhile with genuine designer clothes.

FOOD & DRINK

Local delicacies make particularly suitable presents, such as the wonderfully mild olive oil from Lake Garda. The best (and cheapest) place to buy it is at a cooperative, for example in Gargnano or Limone. There are also very good olive-based products at the Olive Museum in Cisano near Bardolino. Alternatives are high-quality or unusual kinds of pasta, wine and grappa, though the latter two are best bought in supermarkets or specialist wine retailers rather than souvenir shops.

The packaging may be pretty and appealing to tourists, but the contents are not necessarily the best.

SPORTS GEAR

With so many sporting types in the Lake Garda area, there is no shortage of suitable sports shops. In Torbole, windsurfers will find everything they need for their sport, from flashy boards and state-of-the-art equipment to waterproof clothing. Climbers and walkers are catered for especially in Arco, while mountain bikers can get spare parts in Riva or Arco. However, cheap it won't be – you can probably get everything for much less from major sports shops back home.

THE PERFECT ROUTE

THE ALPINE NORTH

In ① *Riva* → p. 41 and *Torbole* → p. 46 is where sports fans in particular will feel at home. Here you can surf, climb, go mountain biking, hike – or watch others. The north shore of the lake is very alpine in character with sheer cliff faces – although Riva boasts a long and beautiful beach as well. ② *Malcesine* → p. 36 huddles close to the shore. The town lies in the shadow of its imposing castle and of course Monte Baldo, which can be reached by cable-car (photo, left). If you have enough time, you can also spend the night at the top.

TAKE A BOAT TO GARDA

A boat trip down the east coast is lovely. You should alight in ③ *Torri del Benaco* → p. 67 with its pretty harbour or in ④ *Garda* → p. 56, at the latest. Its long promenade is the perfect place to go for a stroll and, thanks to the large number of hotels, you can usually find a room even at short notice.

WINE & MORE

It is not a pure coincidence that ⑤ *Bardolino* → p. 51 lent its name to a wine – the village is surrounded by vineyards on the gentle slopes that beg to be explored on foot. In ⑥ *Lazise* → p. 61 time runs slowly. This is where you'll be able to take a deep breath before immersing yourself in the hive of activity in one of the famous ⑦ leisure parks → p. 108/09.

THE LIVELY SOUTH SHORE

⑧ *Peschiera* → p. 64 Barracks and fortresses are witnesses to this area's strategic location in days of old. And it is still readily accessible today. From here, a day trip to Verona by train is a pleasure. ⑨ *Sirmione's* → p. 76 unique situation at the end of a peninsula asks to be visited by boat. From where you disembark, the Grotto of Catullus (*Grotte di Catullo*; photo, right) is the most important Roman excavation on the lake. If you stay the night in Sirmione, you'll be able to experience its charm without all the day-tourists. ⑩ *Desenzano* → p. 70, in the far south west corner, is the largest town on the lake and offers a correspondingly broad range of shops and places to go in the evening.

Experience the different facets of the area by taking a clockwise route around Lake Garda with a few small detours to interesting place

THE SOPHISTICATED WEST SHORE

The west shore is particularly popular among Italian holiday-makers. ⑪ *Salò* → p. 90 is especially good for shopping. It also has the longest lakeside promenade. Tourism on the lake first started in ⑫ *Gardone Riviera* → p. 81: it was where the first hotel was built – a 'grand hôtel' built by a German. Other palatial hotels followed and this is still where the more genteel clientele tend to stay, enjoying walks in the old parks and along the lakeside promenade. In André Heller's giardino you'll find modern art among ancient trees. The twin town ⑬ *Toscolano-Maderno* → p. 85 spreads out around the point where the Toscolano enters the lake. Even as far back as the 14th century, heavy machines could be heard turning rags into a pulp for the paper factories that had been set up along the length of this stream. A walk up-stream into the Valle delle Cartiere is delightful. The countryside around ⑭ *Gargnano* → p. 86 is gentle and soothing. The village is one of the especially quiet corners of the lake. There is not much going on here – and that's just what the visitors want. They enjoy a relaxed time sitting in one of the few cafés on the shore.

SPECTACULAR FINISH

⑮ *Tremosine* → p. 90, high above the lake on a plateau, offers hikers a broad range of choice. In the village of Pieve, a visit to one of the terraces perched high above the lake with plunging views, is a

Time: about four days.
Detailed map of the route on the back cover, in the road atlas and the pull-out map.

must. Slightly further north the lake becomes increasingly narrow and ⑯ *Limone* → p. 32 and *Campione* → p. 88 fight for space with the sheer cliffs that rise steeply behind them. Charming Limone can best be marvelled at when approached by boat.

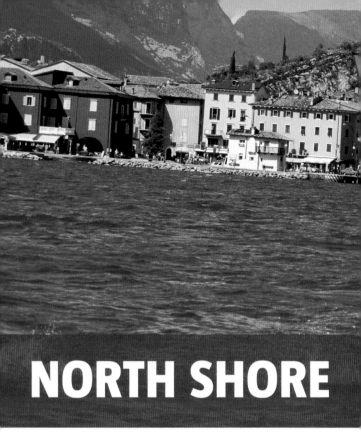

NORTH SHORE

You can skip that trip to a distant fjord in Norway – go to the north end of Lake Garda instead, which has the same spectacular feel. The huge sheer mountain faces leave little room for settlements.

Riva del Garda is the only place with room for growth, since it is situated on the former alluvial plain of the river Sarca. The neighbouring village of Torbole is hemmed in between Monte Brione, the lake shore and the bluff on which the ruins of Penede castle are perched. This situation is what visitors value about Torbole – it creates a wind channel through which the *ora*, *peler* and *balì* winds regularly blow, much to the enjoyment of the surfing community.

Further south you come to the pretty little village of Malcesine which is, however, often overcrowded. Keen climbers ascend the almost 2000-m-high (6500 ft) peak of Monte Baldo towering over the lake. Directly opposite Malcesine is Limone which sometimes seems to groan under the throng of day trippers. The charm of the little place is best savoured early in the morning.

LIMONE

(130 B5) *(ℳ H–I3)* **High mountains loom over the west side of the north end, dropping steeply into the lake.**

Photo: Surfers with Torbole in the background

A paradise for surfers and mountain bikers: a narrow strip of land along the lake and spectacular scenery

Buildings jostle for room in the small Old Town, and people crowd the narrow streets between them. The population is only about 1100, but Limone is nonetheless one of the most popular resorts on Lake Garda. Arriving by boat is the best way to get there, since that's the only way you get to see the remains of the many *limonaie* where lemons were once grown.

In the 18th century, those on a 'grand tour' of Europe marvelled at the lemons and the *limonaie* – the glasshouses. In 1786, the German writer Johann Wolfgang von Goethe noted: "We passed through Limone whose gardens up the side of the mountain, laid out in terraces and planted with lemon trees, looked productive and orderly." The systematic cultivation of lemons on Lake Garda dates back to the 13th century and, in more modern times, costly greenhouses were built to protect the sensitive plants from the frost at night.

The best view of Limone is from the water – arrive by boat!

In winter, they were boarded up by slotting planks into fixed posts. Nowadays, few *limonaie* still operate as it has become uneconomical. In 1861, Lombardy – to which the west shore of Lake Garda belongs – became part of Italy. The border became obsolete and with it, customs duty. Lemons from Sicily could then be bought in northern Italy more cheaply than local ones grown as such expense. By the time the English writer D.H. Lawrence arrived on Lake Garda in 1912, the *limonaie* had been deserted, the posts stuck out of the ground like "the ruins of some temple ... like the final traces of a great race, a forgotten cult."

Shortly before the end of World War I, the Italian government indirectly put an end to the Lake Garda lemon. It had all the protective wooden boards confiscated so that huts could be built quickly for the Italian army up in the mountains. Ten years later there was a particularly hard winter and virtually all the lemon trees on Lake Garda froze as the no longer had the appropriate protection. Nevertheless, lemons are to be seen everywhere in houses and souvenir shops in Limone. The name of the village actually does not derive from the Italian word *limone* but from the Latin *limes* – a border. Today, the only border is the one between Trentino and Lombardy, but until 1918 this was the border between Austria and Italy.

SIGHTSEEING

CASA NATALE DI
SAN DANIELE COMBONI
Daniel Comboni (1831–81) founded the Comboni Missionaries in Africa. In 2003 he was canonised by Pope John Paul II. An exhibition on the life and work of the Roman Catholic missionary can be

seen in the house where Comboni was born. *Daily 9.30am until noon and 3pm until 6.30 | 2 euros | Via Campaldo 18 | www.combonianilimone.it*

LA LIMONAIA DEL CASTEL

The *limonaia* has now been restored and 50 citrus fruit trees planted, ranging from Seville oranges to citrons. *April–Oct daily 10am–6pm, Nov–March Sat/Sun 1pm–4pm | clearly signposted in the town*

SAN BENEDETTO

Originally there was a Roman basilica here. The parish church was built on its ruins in 1691. Don't miss the three 17th-century altarpieces. *Sun 8am–6pm*

SAN PIETRO IN OLIVETO

'St Peter in the Olive Grove' – this small chapel made of uncut boulders is south of the Old Town above Gardesana. The Romanesque church with its single nave is, however, seldom open. The Sagra di San Pietro procession on 29 June finishes here. *Sun 8am–6pm*

FOOD & DRINK

HOTEL RISTORANTE ALLA NOCE

Enjoy such dishes as ribbon noodles with chanterelle mushrooms on the terrace with a view of the lake located just a short walk from the Old Town. *Closed Wed | Via Comboni 33 | tel. 03 65 95 40 22 | www.hotelallanoce.com | Budget–Moderate*

HOTEL AL RIO SE'

Regulars have been returning to this small hotel somewhat off the beaten track for decades. It's very quiet on the terrace of the restaurant where you can enjoy a wonderful fillet of trout with fresh sage and butter. *Open daily April–Oct | Via Nova 12 | tel. 03 65 95 41 82 | www.hotelalriose.com | Budget*

SHOPPING

COOPERATIVA AGRICOLA POSSIDENTI OLIVETI ☺

This cooperative of 'olive-grove owners' does not only sell *olio d'oliva extra vergine* but other related products, such as olives and paste. All olives are grown locally. *Via Campaldo 10 and Via IV Novembre 29 | www.oleificiolimonesulgarda.it*

MARKET

Every first and third Tuesday in the month.

★ **Museo Castello Scaligero**
Natural history with a touch of literary genius in Malcesine's Scaliger Castle → p. 37

★ **Funivia and Seggiovia Monte Baldo**
Far-reaching views from the cable-car with panoramic windows and from the summit → p. 40

★ **Spiaggia Sabbioni in Riva**
One of the largest and most beautiful beaches on the lake with unrestricted public access → p. 44

★ **Cascata del Varone**
The waterfall is the perfect place to take children even if it's raining → p. 45

★ **Museo di Arte Moderna Contemporanea**
20th and 21st-century modern Italian art in Mario Botta's spectacular museum building in Rovereto → p. 101

LEISURE, SPORT & BEACHES

There is a tiny pebbly beach at the north end of the promenade in the Old Town, and the *Spiaggia del Tifù* with beach volleyball on the southern fringe. South of the large carpark you will find the large public pebbly beach. Circolo *Vela Limone (tel. 03 65 91 40 45 | cvlimone@ tiscali.it)* runs sailing courses for old and young.

Every Sunday from June until September a **INSIDER** guided hike takes you to the Bonaventura Segala mountain hut. Meet at 8am in the Bar Turista. Free of charge. It is a challenging hike with a difference in altitude of some 1000 m. A less demanding hike along the sunny path to Ramol is organised on Tuesdays. Meet at 9am in the Bar Turista. A flyer can be downloaded under *www.visitlimonesul garda.com*

ENTERTAINMENT

INSIDER **LA CANTINA DEL GATO BORRACHO**
This *enoteca* (wine shop) is not in the Old Town but on the other side of the through road, next to the multi-storey carpark. Young locals meet here for a glass of wine late evenings. *Closed Tue | Via Caldogno 1 | tel. 0 36 51 98 64 41 | www. gatoborracho.com*

WHERE TO STAY

GARDA
A camping site with a private beach. *Via IV Novembre 10 | located in Fasse sul Lago | tel. 03 65 95 45 50*

LE PALME
If living right in the centre is what you want, this is the place. Le Palme occupies a 17th-century villa. *30 rooms | Via Porto 32 | tel. 03 65 95 46 81 | www. sunhotels.it | Expensive*

RESIDENCE RONCHI
This little complex of holiday flats with a communal pool is situated above the village in the olive groves. Lovely views over the lake. Just 500 m from the centre. *8 flats | Via Milanesa 3 a | tel. 03 65 95 46 96 | www.appartamentironchi.com | Moderate*

HOTEL SOLE
Right plum in the middle of the village, directly on the lakeside and just a hop, skip and jump from where the boats come in – and with a view like in an oil painting. Make sure you ask for a room with a view of the lake! *38 rooms | Via G. Marconi 36 | tel. 03 65 95 40 55 | www. hotelsolelimone.com | Budget–Moderate*

INFORMATION

Via IV Novembre 29 | tel. 03 65 91 89 87 | www.visitlimonesulgarda.com, www.riviera deilimoni.it

MALCESINE

(130 B5–6) (𝄢 I4) Malcesine is the only sizeable village on the east shore at the northern end of the lake. With a population of 3600, it is almost a small town.
The narrow alleys of the Old Town lead up towards the castle. If you only walk along the shore, you miss some of the atmosphere of the place – the streets still harbour tranquil nooks and crannies. Don't miss Scaliger Castle on any account. For one thing, you'll be following the footsteps of the great German writer Johann Wolfgang von Goethe, and there's also a wonderful view of the lake and the rooftops from here.

MUSEO CASTELLO SCALIGERO ★ ●

The museum in the castle has been carefully modernised at great expense. The part in the Palazzo Inferiore of 1620 in the lowest courtyard has a display on

daily 9.30am–7pm, Nov–March Sat/Sun 11am–4pm

PALAZZO DEI CAPITANI DEL LAGO

The palace by the port was built by the Scaligers in the 13th century – the unmistakable design of the battlements

Exhilarating views of Malcesine can be enjoyed from the battlements of Scaliger Castle

the flora, fauna and geology of Monte Baldo, explaining how the Venetians hauled galleys overland to Lake Garda in the 15th century. The Goethe Room has copies of his drawings of Lake Garda. Goethe unpacked his paints and brushes inside the castle and nearly got arrested as a result. He was taken for a Habsburg spy who was not only interested in the castle's appearance but also in its use as a military stronghold. When he told the guards he was from Frankfurt, everything turned out well. *Castle open April–Oct daily 9am–7pm, Feb./March Sat/Sun 12.30pm–6pm, Dec–Early Jan daily 10.30am–4.30pm; Museum April–Oct*

was borrowed from the Venetians and, in the late 15th century, governors from Venice lived here. Nowadays it serves as the Town Hall. Exhibitions are put on from time to time which is a good opportunity to visit a INSIDER**TIP** fine building and the small palm garden directly on the lake.

FOOD & DRINK

INSIDER**TIP** GELATERIA CENTO PER CENTO

This little ice-cream parlour just by the entrance to the castle magically draws every tourist, but locals claim that they themselves often beat a path up the steep road to it because Fabrizio produces the best ice around. *Via Castello 31*

DA PEDRO
If you actually track it down (it's rather tucked away), you will probably recognise the owner from the beach where there's a snack bar of the same name. The place is furnished like an old-fashioned pizzeria and the pizzas are delicious. *Closed Tue | Vicolo Porto Vecchio 9 | tel. 04 57 40 10 81 | Budget–Moderate*

RE LEAR
One of the classier places to eat in Malcesine. You sit under a vaulted ceiling without it being at all rustic; very cosy overlooking the little square to the front. The gourmet *table d'hôte* costs 45 euros and is money well spent. *Closed Tue | Piazza Cavour 23 | tel. 04 57 40 06 16 | www.relear.com | Expensive*

SHOPPING

INSIDER TIP CONSORZIO OLIVICOLTORI ☺
550 smallholders from Malcesine send their olives here for processing. The shop also stocks other local products. *Via Navene 5 | www.oliomalcesine.com*

MARKET
Every Sat morning in the *square by the Municipio.*

NODARI CASALINGHI
This is not one of your ordinary shops for pottery souvenirs, but a very well-stocked place specialising in household utensils – with a few ceramic bowls as well. *Corso Garibaldi 57*

LEISURE, SPORT & BEACHES

A safe footpath and cycle path leads to Navene, 5 km (3 mi) to the north, so the beaches are easy to reach. There is a tiny bathing area beneath the castle, plus a sunbathing area south of the promenade. The business renting mountain bikes (from 20 euros a day) also has flats to rent in the same building at the bottom of the cable-car: *Bike Xtreme | Via Navene Vecchia*

10 and Via Panzano 10 | in nearby Panzano | tel. 04 57 40 01 05 | www.bikeapartments. com.

Tandem paragliding from Monte Baldo can be booked with the pilots directly: *Fabio (tel. 34 97 37 71 94), Mirko (tel. 34 94 28 06 79), Peter (tel. 33 81 95 38 22) and Colman (tel. 33 83 92 24 12).*

ENTERTAINMENT

Malcesine's Old Town is bursting with life in summer until midnight. Like the day trippers earlier on in the day, in the evening night-owls fill the streets.

ART CAFÉ

If you want a change from wine and the usual alcoholic drinks, have a milk shake in the smart Art Café instead. *Piazza Turazza 12*

INSIDER TIP OSTERIA SANTO CIELO

A small *osteria* patronized almost exclusively by young locals. You can get light dishes here, for example *bruschette* or a cheese platter, but the extensive wine list is more notable. The Dutch owner, Hella, fell in love with Italy and stayed on because of the cuisine. *Piazza Turazza 11 | www. osteriasantocielo.com*

PUB VAGABONDO

Here, cyclists and kite-surfers swap banter about wind and wild rides until 3am. Lots of locals, too. *Via Porta Orientale 1*

WHERE TO STAY

CAMPSITES

On the lakeside road in the direction of Navene there is one campsite after another: *Alpino | tel. 04 57 40 04 72 | www. campingalpino.com; Tonino | tel. 04 57 40 13 41 | www.campingtonini.com; Panorama | tel. 04 56 58 41 19*

A dream: the exciting descent from Monte Baldo down to the lakeside

INSIDER TIP HOTEL DU LAC

A newish, small and elegant hotel. The rooms have huge panoramic windows facing the lake. The hotel is directly on the promenade, modern in design and impeccable in style. *36 rooms | Via Gardesana 63 | tel. 04 57 40 01 56 | www.dulac.it | Expensive*

MODENA

A cyclists' hotel in the village centre with a bike room and information for their owners. The accommodation has been renovated in a modern but simple style. *30 rooms | Corso Garibaldi 2 | tel. 04 57 40 00 16 | www.hotelmalcesine.com | Budget*

VILLA ALBA

Some of the rooms have splendid views of the lake. The owner is a motorbike fan. There's space for the bikes in the garage, a high-pressure cleaner and tools – and an extensive breakfast buffet. *12 rooms | Via Gardesana 196 | tel. 04 57 40 02 77 | www.hotelvillaalba.it | Budget–Moderate*

INFORMATION

Via Capitanato 6/8 | tel. 04 57 40 08 37 | www.malcesinepiu.it

OUTINGS

BRENZONE

(134–135 C–D1) (*m* H–I 4–5)

If you head south along the lake, it's not far to Brenzone which is really a collection of villages between Malcesine and Torri del Benaco. Along the shore are Castelletto, the main village of Magugnano, Porto and Assenza, with Borago, Prada and a few others up the slope. From Prada and Costabella, lifts take you up Monte Baldo. Stroll through the narrow streets of ◢┗ *Castello di Brenzone* – it's much more peaceful here than down by the lake and the views of the west shore are fantastic.

South of Castelletto, it's worth stopping for a look at the small church of San Zeno dating from the 11th-century. The *Museo del Lago (Tue–Sun, in winter only Sun 10am until noon and 3pm–6pm)* on the harbour in Cassone has everything to do with fishing on Lake Garda. The building was once used as a fish farm with eels swimming in the outdoor basin. One of the largest diving centres on the lake can also be found in *Assenza di Brenzone: Athos Diving | Via Gardesana 54 | tel. 04 56 59 00 15 | www.athos-diving.com*

You can spend the night in Brenzone at the *Sorriso hotel (26 rooms | Porto di Brenzone | tel. 04 57 42 00 14 | Budget).* It's noisy on the street side, so ask for a room facing the mountains. Directly on the beach is the *Belfiore hotel (32 rooms | Porto di Brenzone | tel. 04 57 42 01 02 | www.consolinihotels.it | Expensive).*

Information: *Via Zanardelli 38 | tel. 04 57 42 00 76 | www.brenzone.it*

EREMO SANTI BENIGNO E CARO ◢┗

(130 B6) (*m* I4)

The hermitage of the Blessed Benignus and Carus is in Cassone. It can be reached by a two-hour walk from the middle station of the cable-car from Malcesine. The path is signposted and easy to find. The church is only open a few days a year. Processions from Malcesine take place on 12 April, 27 July, 16 August and on the third Sunday in October.

FUNIVIA UND SEGGIOVIA MONTE BALDO ★ ◢┗ (130 B–C5) (*m* I4)

The Monte Baldo cable-car climbs 1700 m (5500 ft) from Malcesine via the middle station of San Michele to the summit. That's a double treat since you get a lot of time to look at the view as well as a ride. The cabins are glazed all round and turn on their own axis.

Once at the top, walkers not only have an extensive network of ◢┗ paths with plenty of views to choose from, there's also a level panoramic path – an easy half-hour stroll – with tremendous views of other hikers further down. As this is a very popular excursion, on some days expect to queue for hours! The only way to avoid the crowds on the mountain top is to get up early and catch one of the earliest cable-cars before the crowds arrive. Mountain bikes may also be taken, taking view of the lake from one of the six rooms *(Budget–Moderate)*! *Cable-car daily 8am–5/6/7pm depending on the season | return fare 18, one-way 12, with a mountain bike 16 euros | tel. 04 57 40 02 06 | www.funiviedelbaldo.it*

Monte Baldo always offers spectacular panoramic views and is the perfect place for a rest

but only at specified times in the mornings and afternoons. A chair lift has now opened on the Prà Alpesina plateau for skiers (also open in the peak summer season). The INSIDER TIP *Baita dei Forti (daily | tel. 04 57 40 03 19 | www.baitadei forti.com | Budget–Moderate)* is just a few paces from the summit of the cable-car – a popular place to eat among hikers and skiers. Dishes include the *Trittico Baldo* – a spicy trio of goulash, venison and mushroom ragout served with polenta with a baked cheese topping. What a lot of people don't know is that you can also stay the night here and enjoy a breath-

RIVA DEL GARDA

MAP INSIDE BACK COVER
(130 C3) (Ø I2) With a population of approx. 16,000, Riva is the second-largest town on the lake. Visitors tend to be rather more of a mixed crowd than in the neighbouring surfing mecca of Torbole.
Windsurfers do come to Riva as well, even if the wind conditions are not as favourable for the really fanatical or ambitious

types. Thanks to the long beach and the extensive promenade park, families with children are as well-catered for here as older visitors.

Riva is at the fjord-like northern end of the lake and the town is steadily expanding across the flat alluvial plain of the Sarca. However, the historic Old Town is by the lake. Three town gates – Porta Bruciata, Porta San Marco and Porta San Michele – still exist, marking the start of the Old Town. Every year the pedestrian precinct is extended a little bit more, so that now almost all the Old Town is traffic-free. Guided tours around the town are available free of charge through the tourist information office.

Inviolata Church: plain exterior with rich Baroque interior

The Romans did not fail to recognise the strategic value of the northern end of the lake. Later, in Habsburg times, the town attracted writers and philosophers, including such famous names as Friedrich Nietzsche and Thomas Mann, Rainer Maria Rilke and Franz Kafka. Riva became part of a united Italy at the end of World War I.

SIGHTSEEING

CHIESA DELL'INVIOLATA
The striking octagonal church was built outside the Old Town in the 17th century. It is considered the finest Baroque church in Trentino.

PALAZZO MUNICIPALE
The Venetians built the Town Hall in 1475–82 – something that you cannot really fail to recognise even today as Venetian lion adorns the façade. The Hebrew tombstone of the rabbi Jacopo da Marcaria has been set into a wall under the arcades; his printing workshop was originally on this site.

ROCCA UND MUSEO CIVICO
In the 12th century there was a moated castle here, which the Scaligers turned into a mighty fortress in 1370. The *municipal museum (open end of March–June and in Oct Tue–Sun, July–Sept daily 10am–12.30pm and 1.30pm–6pm | www.comune.rivadelgarda.tn.it/museo)* is now housed on three floors of the castle. The rooms display paintings and interesting aspects of the town's history. There is also an archaeological section.

TORRE APPONALE
The town's 34-m-high (111 ft) landmark that makes pictures of Riva so unmistakable, was built in the 13th century to protect the harbour. The busy Piazza III

Novembre, the heart of the Old Town, spreads out at the foot of the tower.

FOOD & DRINK

RISTORANTE ALPINO
The tables are covered with red-and-white chequered tablecloths and farm workers and bankers alike lunch here on regional specialities such as polenta with venison. The owner also has holiday flats at reasonable prices for his guests *(www.casaalpino.it)*. *Open daily, except Sun in the low season | Via Cerere 10 | tel. 04 64 55 22 45 | Budget*

COMMERCIO
The furnishing of the huge rooms of this old *palazzo* is rustic, but sitting outside is also pleasant. Either way, the home-made lasagne and risotto with a glass of Teroldego, a local red wine, taste just as good. *Closed Mon | Piazza Garibaldi 4 | tel. 04 64 52 17 62 | Moderate*

INSIDER TIP LA MONTANARA
The chequered tablecloths go with the rustic cuisine, such as Trentino horse steaks or *penne* with *taleggio* cheese. *Closed Weds | Via Montanara 20 | tel. 04 64 55 48 57 | Budget*

NUOVO NOVECENTO
The 'Novecento' was one of the most traditional and elegant restaurants in Riva – the 'New Novecento' is a chic winebar with a sophisticated cuisine. Furnished with designer pieces inside, the small but idyllic terrace outside has been left as it was. *Closed Wed and at lunchtime | Via Gazzoletti 6 | tel. 04 64 03 09 00 | Moderate–Expensive*

OSTERIA PANE E SALAME
Davide and Federica Seghetto's tiny *osteria* to the west of the Old Town serves only cheese and salami platters, but the atmosphere is very cosy, and anyway, who needs a full meal every evening? *Closed Mon | Via Marocco 8 | tel. 33 87 40 31 17 | Budget*

SHOPPING

ALIMENTARI MORGHE 😊
Pasta and rice, vegetables, coffee, olives – this shop has everything you'd expect of an Italian grocer – except that INSIDER TIP everything here is organic. And for those who like dark bread, there's wholemeal as well. *Viale Rovereto 101*

Organic perfection: Alimentari Morghe

ERRELUCE
All the smart designer lamps that cost a bomb back home are not exactly cheap here either, but this small shop outside the Old Town also has goods at reduced prices. *Viale dei Tigli 21c*

LIBRERIA IL MAPPAMONDO
The bookshop not only has prettier postcards than most but foreign-language books as well, for those long days on the beach. *Via Disciplini 30*

MARKET
In summer, the market is held every second and fourth Wed of the month in *Viale Dante*.

Riva has one of the largest and best public beaches on the whole lake. The ★ *Spiaggia Sabbioni* runs from next to the harbour towards Torbole, as far as Monte Brione. Lots of shade, a variety of bars and ice-cream kiosks.

There are several places to rent bikes for those without their own; specialist outlets also have mountain bikes for the more sporty as well as conventional bikes: *The Lab Bike Wellness (Via G. Carducci 8 b | www.the-lab.it); Bikes Girelli (Viale Damiano Chiesa 15/17); Cicli Pederzolli (Viale dei Tigli 24 | www.pederzolli.it).*

Surfing and sailing schools can be found dotted along the beach from the harbour in Riva to the outskirts of Torbole.

But you don't always have to jump on a mountain bike or surf board. For those who want to keep supple while on holiday, just book a ● yoga course: *Ruurd Reelick & Monica Burri Reelick | tel. 34 05 11 62 94 | www.yogaintegralegarda.org*

ENTERTAINMENT

INSIDER TIP ▶ BINARIO

Smartly-dressed night-owls meet frequent this restaurant near the marina. *Closed Tue | Largo Medaglie d'Oro al Valor Militare 2 | www.restaurantcafebinario.it*

CAFÉ LATINO

Evening venue next to the hydro-electric power station for dancing and chilling out. *Fri/Sat from 8pm | Via Monte Oro 14*

You'll find the most suitable clothing for the beach and sport at the various markets around the lake such as here in Riva

JONNY'S PUB/ IL VECCHIO PORTO
Loud music and beer attract the local youth scene to these two bars. *Piazza Catena 5 and 7*

HOTEL ANCORA
This little hotel right in the middle of the pedestrian precinct is furnished in the Art Deco style. The restaurant terrace is equally pretty. *14 rooms | Viale Dante 47 | tel. 04 64 56 70 99 | www.rivadelgarda. com/ancora | Moderate*

HOTEL ASTORIA
Elegant but unpretentious, this is the most modern hotel in town and boasts a large spa complex. *100 rooms | Viale Trento 9 | tel. 04 64 57 66 57 | www.relax hotels.com | Expensive*

OSTELLO BENACUS
Three-storey youth hostel with two twin rooms and two rooms with four bed, each with their own bathrooms, as well as dormitories with lockers. *Piazza Cavour 14 | tel. 04 64 55 49 11 | www.ostelloriva.com | Budget*

AGRITURISMO EDEN MARONE & AGRITUR GIRARDELLI
This family-run business has always been a firm favourite. A few years ago the two brothers Tiziano and Walter open a second building: Agritur Girardelli, which has its own jacuzzi and sauna, is just below Eden Marone. Price includes INSIDER TIP conducted mountain bike tours organised by a local specialist! *Marone: 15 rooms | Via Marone 11 | tel. 04 64 52 15 20 | www.edenmarone.it | Budget; Girardelli: 8 rooms | Via Marone 8 | Tel. 04 64 52 16 42 | www.agriturgirardelli.it | Budget–Moderate*

VILLA MARIA
This small guest house within walking distance of the Old Town is quiet if you take a room at the back. The rooms are modestly furnished, but the service makes up for that. *10 rooms | Viale dei Tigli 19 | tel. 04 64 55 22 88 | www.garnimaria.com | Budget*

Largo Medaglie d'Oro al Valor Militare | tel. 04 64 55 44 44 | fax 04 64 52 03 08 | www. gardatrentino.it

CASCATA DEL VARONE ★
(130 B3) (*m I2*)
What peacefully shimmers up in Lago di Tenno drops 100 m (330 ft) here into the valley below with a roar. The ● Varone waterfall 5 km (3 mi) north of Riva was opened to visitors in 1874. *March and Oct daily 9am–5pm, April and Sept 9am–6pm, May–Aug 9am–7pm, Nov–Feb Sun 10am–5pm | www.cascata-varone.com*

LAGO DI LEDRO
(130 A–B3) (*m H2*)
If it gets too hot or too crowded for you down on Lake Garda, you can take a shortish 10-km trip (6 mi) into the mountains. After passing through two long tunnels, you reach the high plain of the *Valle di Ledro* (www.vallediledro.com), and soon after lake Ledro. At the far end is the *Lido* hotel with a lovely beach *(34 rooms | Pieve di Ledro | tel. 04 64 59 10 37 | www.hotel lidoledro.it | Moderate–Expensive)*.
In *Locanda Tre Oche (closed Mon | Molina di Ledro | Via Maffei 37 | tel. 04 64 50 90 62 | www.treoche.it | Moderate)* you should try the typical Trentino specialities such as barley soup or homemade pasta. The restaurant also has rooms.

ROMAN EXCAVATIONS, SAN MARTINO (130 B3) (⫿⫿ I2)

These excavations are rather out-of-the-way, a few kilometres north-west of *Campi*. You can leave your car at the church and follow the waymarked path to the archeological site on foot through the woods (30 mins) or, alternatively, go straight to a car park a little bit nearer. The remains are of a Roman house, with possibly a shrine built on still older walls.

TENNO AND LAGO DI TENNO (130 B2–3) (⫿⫿ I2)

Tenno is a favourite destination for trippers holidaying in the northern Lake Garda area. A winding road leads 6 km (4 mi) uphill. From Tenno, you can take a delightful walk along the *Sentiero del Salt* to the *Canale di Tenno*, a well looked-after medieval village.

Go a few kilometres further into the mountains and you come to Lago di Tenno, a dark-green mountain lake with a small beach. For over-night stays, there is the *Clubhotel Lago di Tenno (38 rooms, 31 flats | tel. 04 64 50 20 31 | www.club hoteltenno.com | Moderate)*.

TORBOLE

(130 C2–3) (⫿⫿ I2) **Torbole is the youngest place on the lake. That's not from a historical point of view – Torbole is where the youthful, keen sporty types meet up, and most of these are surfers.**

Even for ambitious, skilled surfers the winds on Lake Garda offer near-perfect conditions. In the evenings, the pubs of Torbole likewise offer plenty of entertainment, which at the week-ends goes on into the small hours.

The double commune Torbole-Nago (population 2300) is part of Trentino. You get the best view of the lake by driving down the road from Nago and stopping at the carpark after the hairpin bend at the Ice Age glacial formations, the *Marmitte dei Giganti*.

SIGHTSEEING

CASA BEUST

The distinctive red house in the port was once popular with artists. Around the turn of the 20th century an art school focussing on painting from life was established.

CASELLO DAZIO

The light yellow building on the harbour that stands slightly apart from everything else, is the former Austrian customs house. The Habsburger's built it on the Venetian wooden piles used to create the jetty.

SANT'ANDREA ☀

The 12th century church that was remodelled in the Baroque period has an elevated position with a beautiful view over the lake. A sunclock can be seen on the south wall. The altarpiece from 1741 by Giambettino Cignaroli depicting Saint Andrew's martyrdom is well worth seeing.

FOOD & DRINK

CA' ROSSA

A rustic eatery on the other side of the Sarca, located in Linfano. The fish baked in bread dough is particularly good. *Closed Wed | Via Linfano 45 | tel. 04 64 50 58 58 | Budget–Moderate*

CASA BEUST

3.50 euros for a tiny *spremuta* (freshly pressed orange juice) might be a bit steep – but that's the price you have to pay if you want the best place to watch the surfers. Prices of the fish dishes are standard. *Closed Weds | Via Benaco 13 | tel. 04 64 50 55 76 | Moderate*

As Mediterranean the surfer mecca Torbole may feel, its surroundings are definitely alpine

HOTEL CENTRALE

The food here is excellent, whether it's fish or just a pizza. Sitting under a wide awning overlooking the piazza is also very pleasant. *Closed Wed | Piazza Goethe 13 | tel. 04 64 50 52 34 | www.hotelcentrale torbole.it | Moderate*

SURFERS GRILL

Hungry surfers know it already: they besiege this restaurant, where – as the name says – grilled dishes are the speciality. *Closed Mon | Via Sarca Vecchio 5 | tel. 04 64 50 59 30 | www.surfersgrill.it | Moderate*

LA TERRAZZA

This classier restaurant is nicest in the evenings. The fish specialities (unfortunately none too cheap) are a good accompaniment to the wonderful sunset (free of charge). Reserve early. *Closed Tue | Via Benaco 14 | tel. 04 64 50 60 83 | www. allaterrazza.com | Expensive*

VILLA CIAN

Its pizza and pasta and the brilliant view of the lake tend to attract a younger public. Lots of partying. *Closed Tue | Via Foci del Sarca 11 | tel. 04 64 50 52 54 | www. villaciantorbole.it | Moderate*

LEISURE, SPORT & BEACHES

A long beach of small pebbles stretches from near the town centre to the River Sarca. Bike rental companies are just as well represented in Torbole as surf courses and places to hire boards, such as the *Windsurfing Center Conca d'Oro (www. windsurfconca.com)* and *Vasco Renna Surf (www.vascorenna.com)* in the marina and *Surf-Segnana (Foci del Sarca | www.surf-segnana.it)*.

You can take a shady walk starting at the parish church. ● *Via Santa Lucia* goes all the way to Nago – and uncovers an important era in the area's history. In a particularly bold campaign in the 15th century, the Venetians transported their warships over the mountains and reached the water at Torbole by following the Via Santa Lucia. In 1439 battles were fought on the lake against Milan.

A more INSIDER TIP demanding walk takes a route above Torbole parallel to the shore and will lead you southwards to Tempesta in around three hours. Although this is not a fixed-rope route, clambering up and down metal ladders and steps in the cliff face does demand a head for heights. The return journey can be done by bus.

ENTERTAINMENT

Surfers congregate in early evening around the tables outside on the Piazza Vittorio Veneto. Later, they move into the bars in the town. There's live music every Friday at the *Conca d'Oro* disco pub *(Thu–Sun 10pm–4am | Lungolago Verona 2).*

WHERE TO STAY

CAMPING

As windsurfers prefer to shell out for a new board rather than an expensive bed, many of them come in a dormobile or with a tent. For this reason, there are masses of camp sites in Torbole to cater for them, e.g. *Europa (tel. 04 64 50 58 88 | www.campingeuropatorbole.it),* and the more basis sites *Al Cor (tel. 04 64 50 52 22 | www.camping-al-cor.com)* and *Al Porto (tel. 04 64 50 58 91 | www.campingalporto.it).*

CASA BERTOLINI

Flats with one or several rooms are available in three different buildings all of which are close to the beach. Modern INSIDER TIP Casa 3 is particularly attractive, located on the bank of the Sarca in a park. *Via Pasubio 12 | tel. 04 64 50 52 77 | www.casabertolini.com | Moderate*

GEIER

Situated directly beside the former Venetian port. Behind the hotel is a small, quiet garden. *37 rooms | Via Benaco 15 | tel. 04 64 50 51 31 | www.hotelgeier.com | Moderate*

LIDO BLU

The perfect situation of the hotel beside the mouth of the Sarca is best appreciated from the lake. So it's no surprise that it's much favoured by surfers. Swimming pool and sauna in the hotel. *40 rooms | Via del Sarca Vecchio 39 | tel. 04 64 50 51 80 | www.lidoblu.it | Expensive*

CLUBHOTEL LA VELA

This is the place to stay if the surfboard is not your only pleasure. The facilities (pool, water massage and sauna) are for sporty types who like luxury. The hotel also has flats to rend. *57 rooms and suites | Via Strada Grande 2 | tel. 04 64 50 59 40 | www.lavelahoteltorbole.it | Moderate–Expensive*

VILLA CLARA

B&B just 200 m from the beach and town centre. Simple rooms, fitness room, small garden, bike and surfboard storage and and a garage for motorbikes. *24 rooms | Via Matteotti 92 | tel. 04 64 50 51 41 | www.villaclara.it | Budget*

INFORMATION

Lungolago Verona 19 | tel. 04 64 50 51 77 | www.gardatrentino.it

OUTINGS

MARMITTE DEI GIGANTI

(130 C3) (*Ø I2*)

Whether the 'Marmitte dei Giganti' look like huge cauldrons from which giants quench their thirst – as the name implies –

is a matter of conjecture. Whatever you want to believe, these glacial hollows – formed in the ice age – are impressive. Water from the melting snows mixed with sand and gravel swirled around at great speed and scooped out these dips in the rock. Such formations can be found below the road from Nago to Torbole. Just after a long left-hand bend you'll come to a carpark on the right. Unfortunately the first 100 m is along the road but then a path branches off downhill. After a good three-minute walk you'll find the cauldrons and can look back at the smooth overhanging rock wall above. A ladder to the right leads to another 'giant's pot'. These rock formations can also be reached on foot from Torbole (approx. 15 mins), by following the Via Strada Granda behind Hotel Vela. The sometimes extreme overhanging cliffs are popular among climbers. It's spectacular watching climbers overcome gravity.

MONTE BRIONE ᨀ
(130 C3) (*ⓜ I2*)
Torbole and Riva are separated by the massive 376-m-high (1233 ft) limestone bluff of Monte Brione. Waymarked trails lead to the top. The most remarkable viewpoint of Lake Garda is from the summit – on top of a bunker built by the Austrians in 1860.

NAGO (130 C3) (*ⓜ I2*)
Signposted left in Nago, which is a continuation of Torbole, is the path to the *castello*, the ᨀ ruins of *Penede Castle.* It was slighted by French troops around 1700 due to its strategically important location. The fortress was only used for military purposes and boasted a gunpowder magazine and watchtower, a Venetian styled bulwark and a drawbridge. From Nago castle, a ᨀ path with panoramic views leads to the restored ruins of the

fortress. A walk along the path alone is worth it for the views.

The more than 100-year-old, traditional ☺ *Eco Hotel Zanella (33 rooms | Via Sighele 1 | tel. 04 64 50 51 54 | www.eco-hotelzanella.com | Budget–Moderate)*, in the centre of the village, has established itself now as an environmentally-friendly hotel. The breakfast table is piled high with local produce; soaps and shower gel are organic and biodegradable. Small pool in the inner courtyard.

The marvel of erosion: the Marmitte dei Giganti

EAST SHORE

The 'East Shore' starts where the car ferries come in, in Torri del Benaco, and extends down through Garda, Bardolino and Lazise to the southernmost point at Peschiera. This part of the lake is known as the 'Olive Riviera'.

The silvery leaves which catch the golden sunlight stretch as far as the eye can see. And wherever there are no olive groves with their dry-stone walls and cut terraces there's bound to be a vineyard. In actual fact, the olive trees are getting fewer and fewer; harvesting is so strenuous that nobody wants the job now.

In the 1960s, the stream of tourists had already started moving south wards – and in some of the more basic hotels you can still get an idea as to what holidaying in Italy must have been like forty years ago. Of course, today, luxurious places to stay in can also be found along the 'Olive Riviera'. But not in the 'grands hôtels' of old, as on the other side of the lake, but in modern complexes with their swimming pools and beauty farms. However, staying in such hotels means being out of the town centres as the settlements along the shore do not to have any room for such hotels. Torri del Benaco is huddled around the old harbour, while Garda is a little more stretched out. Bardolino is the biggest place along this stretch of the shore, and the little lakeside village of Lazise is the last stop on the Gardesana

Photo: The Bardolino wine-growing area

Narrow streets in historic towns and leisure parks: the 'Olive Riviera' on the Venetian side could equally well be called the 'Wine Riviera'

Orientale. The flat beaches in the area have always attracted families and vast leisure parks sprouted up, the best-known of which is Gardaland.

BARDOLINO

MAP INSIDE BACK COVER
(134 C3) (∅ H6) **If someone only knows one place on Lake Garda, then it will probably be Bardolino – the traditional tourist destination.**

And should someone not know Lake Garda at all, then at least this place name may ring a bell: Bardolino is also the name of the wine that grows on the gentle slopes rising up behind the little town which lies towards the southern end of the eastern shore. This stretch of country was settled back in the Bronze Age. The Romans built a town which developed into the

The Cisano olive-oil museum: ancient presses and freshly produced olive oil

self-governing community of Bardolino in the Middle Ages, when it came under the rule of the House of Scaliger. The Old Town in Bardolino (pop. 6700) is larger than that of other towns along the 'Olive Riviera'. The shops in the relatively wide lanes that criss-cross each other, stay open until around midnight. Night and day – except during the siesta in the midday heat – throngs of people stream through the Old Town. The ★ *Piazza Giacomo Matteotti* is alway brimming with life. The square is really a relatively wide street that leads from the neo-Classicist parish church Santi Nicolò e Severo down to the lakeside. This is where you'll find a number of bars, cafés and icecream parlours. And this is where the locals and holiday-makers stroll around in the evenings: *fare le vasche* as the Italian call it – 'doing lengths'.

SIGHTSEEING

MUSEO DELL'OLIO DI OLIVA

2 km (1.9 mi) south of the village of Cisano, near Bardolino, the olive oil museum is the perfect place not just to buy quality oil but also to find out in depth how olive oil is manufactured. Don't miss the video show: *Mon–Sat 9am–12.30pm and 2.30pm–7pm, Sun 9am–12.30pm | Via Peschiera 54 | www.museum.it*

MUSEO DEL VINO

Strictly speaking, it's a bit of a con: a wine merchant has collected a number of old winepresses and bottling plants and now demonstrates the art of wine-making while calling the whole set up a museum. Basically it's a winery with wine-tasting – but it is interesting nevertheless. *Mid March–Oct daily 9am–1pm and 2.30pm–7pm | Via Costabella 9 | www.zeni.it*

SAN SEVERO ★ ●

The small church on the main road was rebuilt in the Romanesque style after the earthquake of 1117. The remains of the previous church, some 300 years older, can still be seen. The faded but largely intact frescos from the first half of the 12th century that once covered the whole interior of this harmoniously designed church are particularly beautiful.

SAN ZENO

This church can easily be missed when driving through Bardolino as it is tucked away in a small courtyard on Via San Zeno on the hill side. Its walls date from the 9th century. This house of prayer – with its narrow, soaring interior and its cross-shaped ground plan – is one of the oldest Carolingian churches in the whole of north-ern Italy. The six unusually large pillars with equally large capitals are striking.

FOOD & DRINK

AL COMMERCIO

In the picturesque inner courtyard you will find a good selection of grilled meat dishes, freshly prepared mixed salads which consist of more than just grated carrots, and a wine list that is also quite respectable. *Closed Tue | Via Solferino 1 | tel. 04 57 211 83 | Moderate*

LA FORMICA

Homemade pasta is served in this little restaurant in the centre – with *ragù* (ra-gout) or truffles for example – and large salads. No view of the lake, but quieter as a consequence. *Closed Mon | Piazza Lenotti 11 | tel. 04 57 211 705 | www.la formica.vr.it | Budget*

IL GIARDINO DELLE ESPERIDI

This restaurant in the Old Town is still a top address. Wine-tasting sessions are sometimes held in the adjoining *enoteca*. *Closed all day on Tue and lunchtime on Wed | Via Mameli 1 | tel. 04 56 210 477 | Expensive*

CAFÉ ITALIA

A chic place to people-watch on the pi-azza. This is where the young people from the area meet. Snacks – polenta, cold meat and cheese platters, *caprese* (toma-toes and mozzarella), as well as fruit – are served to accompany a wide selection of locally produced wines. *Closed Mon | Piazza Principe Amedeo 3–4 | tel. 04 57 211 585 | Budget*

DA MEMO

In this quieter corner of the Old Town, sitting outside is just as nice as inside the 16th-century building. One of the specialities is baked whitefish – a tasty freshwater variety. *Closed Mon | Piazza Statuto 15 | tel. 04 57 210 130 | www. tavernadamemo.com | Moderate*

SHOPPING

INSIDER TIP ▶ LA BARCHESSA ARTE

The trendy crowd is drawn to this desir-able address in the Palazzo Rambaldi, which doubles as a huge gallery space, a bar and a concept store with designer articles. *Via San Martino 28*

MARCO POLO HIGHLIGHTS

★ **Piazza Giacomo Matteotti**
In the evening the piazza in Bardolino come alive → p. 52

★ **San Severo**
Frescos from the early 12th century can be seen in the Romanesque church on the main road in Bardolino → p. 52

★ **Punta San Vigilio**
You can swim in the bay at a price; a cappuccino at the harbour costs a little less → p. 60

★ **Arena di Verona**
The most magnificent Italian operas performed in a less formal atmosphere in the open air in Verona → p. 65

BARDOLINO

CANTINE LENOTTI
This family-run business has been a winery since 1906. Their excellent but not exactly cheap wine goes under the label 'Le Selezioni di Lenotti', but they also have commendable table wines. *Via Santa Cristina 1 | www.lenotti.com*

MARKET
The market is held every Thursday. One of the biggest on the lake, it stretches along the lakeside and into some of the lanes in the Old Town.

LEISURE, SPORT & BEACHES

No swimming directly in the town itself, but to the north and south of the Old Town there are a number of beaches along the shoreline. In the direction of Cisano, there is a rocky beach without any shade but with picnic places on the strips of grass along the beach promenade. The next place to swim nearest to the town centre is *Punta Cornicello*. The small pebbly beach (free of charge) near Via Ugo Foscolo also has a children's playground. If you go further than Punta Cornicello towards Garda, there is a long stretch of beach which can be reached on foot along the path next to the lake. Entrance is free but in most places there is a deep drop.

The cycling paths towards Garda and Lazise are continuously being improved and a short bike trip to a neighbouring village is always worthwhile. Some hotels have bikes to rent or else try: *Bici-Center | Via Marconi 60 | tel. 04 57 21 10 53*

ENTERTAINMENT

CONCERTS
Every Wed in the summer season at 9.30pm, classical music concerts are given on the church steps on the Piazza Matteotti. Classical concerts are held in the church San Severo from July until September.

OSTERIA FRANCISCUS
There are lots of tables outside which means that you can usually find somewhere to sit, at least before 10pm. After that the *osteria* starts to fill up – and is especially popular with the young local crowd. Food is not the main attraction here: there is live music and draught beer. *Closed Mon | Via Verdi 11*

PRIMO LIFE CLUB
Although you can eat here too, it doesn't start to get lively until after midnight. The roof terrace is a wonderful place to sit. *Fri–Sun 9pm–4am | Via Marconi 14 | www.primolifeclub.com*

INSIDER TIP LO STRAMBINO
This is where the not-quite-so-young locals meet either before or after a meal for a glass of wine or perhaps even a piece of pizza on the side. Good value, loud, packed and open until midnight. *Closed Mon | Via Cavour 41 | www.strambino.com*

LOW BUDGET

▶ For the 'Olive riviera' you can benefit from the free *Riviera Card*. This gives you reductions in amusement parks and zoos, on boats and ferries, on the cable-car and on entrance fees to some museums. Just ask in your hotel!

▶ Mountaineering and outdoor clothing can be found at discount prices at the *Salewa Outlet* in Bussolengo *(Tue–Sat 9am–12.30pm and 3pm–7.30pm | Via 1° Maggio 26).*

WHERE TO STAY

CAESIUS THERME & SPA RESORT

This exclusive spa hotel in Cisano has both an indoor and a large outdoor pool and offers a range of Ayurveda treatments. *185 rooms | Via Peschiera 1 | tel. 04 57 21 91 00 | www.hotelcaesiusterme.com | Expensive*

the same name in the building – especially good for fish dishes. *12 rooms | Via San Colombano 11 | tel. 04 57 21 03 48 | Budget*

HOTEL QUATTRO STAGIONI

A large, family-run hotel. Very popular especially since the swimming pool was built in the garden a few years ago. You can't

The Piazza Matteotti is turned into an open-air concert hall on Wednesday evenings in the peak summer season

CISANO

Campers at this site have the choice of several different pools, even though it is right on the lake itself. In Cisano near Bardolino. *Via Peschiera 48 | tel. 04 56 22 90 98 | www.camping-cisano.it*

PENSION MILANI

The rooms may be simple, and some only have a shower-room in the corridor, but you won't find anything much cheaper in Bardolino. And it's clean. Better known than the guesthouse is the restaurant of

get more central than this in Bardolino's Old Town. *36 rooms | Borgo Garibaldi 23 | tel. 04 57 21 00 36 | www.hotel4stagioni. com | Moderate–Expensive*

SAN VITO

Well appointed campsite in Cisano with huge pool, although not directly on the lakeside. *Via Pralesi 3 | tel. 04 56 22 90 26*

AGRITURISMO TRE COLLINE

This family-run business is 5 km (3.1 mi) from Bardolino in the hills further inland.

In addition to a pool and flats there is also an *agricampeggio* – a small camp site among the vineyards. Home-grown or homemade produce – such as their own Bardolino – can be tried on request. *Palù 26 | tel. 04 57 23 52 19 | www.trecolline bardolino.it | Moderate*

OUTINGS

STRADA DEL VINO ●
(134–135 C–D 3–5) (𝄞 H–I 6–8)

A route that one person will not really be able to enjoy very much: the driver … The 'Wine Route' starts just a little to the north of Bardolino and goes through Affi, Pastrengo and Castelnuovo in the direction of Peschiera. With more than 40 winegrowers and producers to visit, you will be able to enjoy a wine shoppping spree and wine tasting. *www.ilbardolino. com/la-strada.html*

LAKESIDE PROMENADE
(134 C3) (𝄞 H6)

The lakeside promenade in Bardolino and towards the south has been turned into a chic boardwalk rather like being on the deck of a ship. A 1-hour walk takes you along the lakeside to Garda. There are a number of beaches along the way so don't forget your swimming gear.

On the outskirts of the town, the path deviates a little from the shore and turns inland. This leads past a red house standing on its own – the municipal meeting place for the the older generation in the area. The building was once Bardolino's station at a time when trains still ran from Verona to Garda.

GARDA

(134 C3) (𝄞 H6) **Garda has a population of 4000 and stretches around the wide bay between Punta San Vigilio and the 'Rocca'.**

Its pretty, traffic-free Old Town is popular among locals and tourists alike as a place to stroll. Along the shore there is one café after another. The lanes in the Old Town are quite narrow and the main streets can get very crowded sometimes. However, if you get away from the shops there are still secret corners to be discovered. In the evening things quieten down and you can sit cosily in the cafés along Lungolago Regina Adelaide.

There really was a real queen once too, Adelaide of Burgundy, who was held prisoner here more than 1000 years ago. As early as 768, Charlemagne had made Garda a county in its own right and from then onwards the lake was named after

this town, and not by its earlier Roman name Benacus. On the Rocca di Garda above the lake there was once a castle where Adelaide was kept captive. Now it is in ruins.

PALAZZO DEL CAPITANO DELLA SERENISSIMA

The Gothic arched windows give it away: this charming *palazzo* dates from Venetian times. It was the seat of the officials from the 'Serenissima' – as Venice is called, who headed the lakeside town council. Originally a harbour was right in front of it, but the basin was filled in and a square created, the Piazza Catullo – to the pleasure of all those on foot today.

ROCCA DI GARDA ⚘

The word 'garda', similar to the English 'guard', is derived from the old German 'wardon' which means 'to observe'. And from this vantage point – the cliff rises up 200 m above the lake – there is a good all-round view. Starting behind the parish church dedicated to Santa Maria Maggiore a waymarked path leads to the fortress, of which only a few remaining walls are still standing. A stone seat that looks rather like a throne is particularly noticeable. It is known locally as 'Adelaide's chair'.

SANTA MARIA MAGGIORE

Garda's parish church is outside the original town walls. It is presumed that the earlier structure on the site, built by the Lombards in the 8th century, was the fortress chapel, as the site is directly below the 'Rocca'. The INSIDER TIP 15th-century cloisters are well worth seeing. *Piazzale Roma*

VILLA ALBERTINI

The dark red villa at the northern approach to the town, with its distinctive crenellated Ghibelline-style towers, cannot be missed.

A host of cafés in Garda's pretty Old Town offer a warm welcome to their guests

GARDA

It can only be viewed from the outside. It was in this palace in 1848 that Charles Albert – the king of Piedmont-Sardinia – received the parliamentary delegation that brought him the charter declaring the annexation of Lombardy to the Kingdom of Piedmont (and, as such, later of Italy).

RISTORANTE GIARDINETTO
Slightly away from the hustle and bustle although directly on the lake, this is the best place for fish dishes such as spaghetti and crab. *Open daily | Lungolago Regina Adelaide 27 | tel. 04 57 25 50 51 | www.zaglio.it | Expensive*

The Villa Albertini, with its distinctive battlements, lies on the outskirts of Garda

FOOD & DRINK

INSIDER TIP AI BEATI
The restaurant is at the top of the hill, reached after turning left off the road to Costermano. The view is stunning, and the food in the converted oil mill is much better and only negligibly more expensive than that in the restaurants down on the lake. *Open noon–2.30pm, 7pm–10.30pm, Sept–June closed at lunchtime on Tue and Wed, July, Aug closed Wed, Thu lunchtime | Via Val Mora 57 | tel. 04 57 25 57 80 | www.ristoranteaibeati.com | Expensive*

AL GRASPO
A hectic place but very Italian. The waiters never stop producing one course after another, mainly seafood and enough wine to see anyone through the evening. Fixed price of 30 euros. *Closed Tue | Piazzetta Calderini 12 | tel. 04 57 25 60 46 | Moderate*

SHOPPING

MARKET
Every Friday morning there is a market on *Lungolago Regina Adelaide*.

LA PESCHERIA ●
Fresh fish from the lake can best be bought at the fish cooperative. *Only 7am–1pm (daily) and 4pm–7pm (daily except Wed and Sun) | Via delle Antiche Mura 8*

LEISURE, SPORT & BEACH

Just to the north of Garda there is a long, narrow pebbly beach which is the favourite haunt of local youths. No entrance charge, hardly any parking spaces. ● Gardacqua is a mixture of outdoor pool, spa and exclusive leisure complex. *Daily 9am–9pm | entrace fee from 8.90 euros | Via Cirillo Salaorni 10 | www.gardacqua.it*

ENTERTAINMENT

INSIDER TIP CERCHIO APERTO
The 'in' place with its mixture of live music, exhibitions or jazz – a brand new, trendy and popular café where young people from the area get together. *Open daily | Piazza Calderini 1 | www.cerchioaperto.com*

PAPILLON
Live music is played in this music bar well into the night – but not on a regular basis. *Closed Tue | Via delle Antiche Mura 26 | www.barpapillon.it*

WHERE TO STAY

PICCOLO HOTEL
The 'little hotel', tucked away in a corner of Garda's historical main square, is housed in an old *palazzo. 10 rooms | Piazza Catullo 11/12 | tel. 04 57 25 52 56 | www.piccolo hotelgarda.it | Budget–Moderate*

TOBAGO
A brand new spa hotel, thoroughly designed interior and a large outdoor pool that is heated in winter. *18 rooms | Via V.*

Bellini 1 | tel. 04 57 25 63 40 | www.garda hotel-zaglio.com | Expensive

TRE CORONE
This hotel was opened in 1860 as a coaching inn and is mentioned in the 1895 edition of Baedeker's. Today it is simply a comfortable, standard-category hotel. Many of the rooms have a view of the lake. *26 rooms | Lungolago Regina Adelaide 54 | tel. 04 57 25 53 36 | www.hoteltrecorone.it | Moderate*

INFORMATION

Piazza Donatori di Sangue 1 | tel. 04 56 27 03 84 | iatgarda@provincia.vr.it

OUTINGS

EREMO DI SAN GIORGIO DELLA ROCCA (134 C3) (*H6*)
On the opposite peak to la Rocca is the 17th-century Camaldolese hermitage that is open to the public. The monastery was dissolved after Napoleon overran the area soon after 1810 and was then occupied by farmers. In 1885 the monks returned. There is a small monastery shop in which herbs, liqueur and oil are sold. Women are not allowed inside the monastery. Men, however, can even stay the night – albeit in spartan accommodation. *Tel. 04 57 21 13 90 | www.eremosangiorgio.it*

ROCK ENGRAVINGS ● (134 B–C3) (*H6*)
The rock engravings around Garda and Torri del Benaco are evidence of the early settlement of this area. Some engravings can be seen by taking a walk from Garda northwards for about an hour. Maps are available from the tourist information office but you don't really need one as the route is clearly signposted. First walk parallel to the beach almost as far as

Punta San Vigilio, then follow the wooden signs marked 'Graffiti' past a park and a short distance along the main road. Turn right into Via Castei where you will find a number of wooden signs pointing to the rock engravings which are not that easy to find. The outline of a 'Nine Men's Morris' game can be seen as well as several matchstick men, although these may well have only been added in the Middle Ages. Historians have great difficulty dating engravings at the best of times. Don't wear open-toed shoes as snakes sometimes like to sunbathe on the path.

ISOLA DEL GARDA (134 A3) (*[0] G6*)
This, the only largish island on Lake Garda, is privately owned. The Saints Francis, Anthony of Padua and Bernardino of Siena are reputed to have lived here, as is even the universally famous Italian poet Dante Alighieri. The picturesque villa on the island was built in the early 20th century in Gothic Revival style. A stroll in the park takes you past exotic trees and between huge cypresses. The island is open to the public from May to October. Every day boats from various places around the lake visit the island, e.g. on Wed from Garda and Bardolino. *Reservation necessary | tel. 32 83 84 92 26 | www.isoladelgarda.com | 24–33 euros).*

ORTO BOTANICO DI MONTE BALDO ☺
(135 E1) (*[0] I5*)
These beautiful botanic gardens were planted on the site of an older forestry garden. No plants were introduced from other climatic zones – INSIDER TIP only indiginous species are to be found here. As such, Monte Baldo's floral diversity can be shown to the full – being an area frequently referred to as the 'garden of Europe.' The gardens can be reached by heading out to Caprino Veronese, then via Spiazzi, Ferrara di Monte Baldo and Novezzina (in total approx. 20 km; 12.4 mi). *May–Sept. Open daily, 9am–6pm | Tours by appointment. Tel. 04 56 24 72 88 | www.ortobotanicomontebaldo.org*

PUNTA SAN VIGILIO ★
(134 B3) (*[0] G6*)
A peninsula lying immediately to the west of Garda. An extensive olive grove follows the curve of the lovely bay – the *Baia delle Sirene (www.parcobaiadellesirene.it)*, where you can bathe – at a price: entrance fee 12 euros. There is also a children's activity programme (5 euros). To the north of this, there is a rather stoney public beach. In 1540, Michele Sanmicheli – an accomplished builder of fortresses – constructed the *Villa Guarienti-Brenzone* on the peninsula. Those who can afford it stay at the *Locanda San Vigilio (7 rooms | tel. 04 57 25 66 88 | www.locanda-sanvigilio.it | Expensive)*. Those on a more modest budget can at least enjoy a cappuccino or a campari here.

SAN ZENO DI MONTAGNA
(134 C2) (*[0] H5*)
A beautiful ☀ panoramic route takes you from Garda via Costermano to the mountain village San Zeno, 25 km (15½ mi) to the north. The journey is especially worthwhile for those who want to wine and dine to perfection. Situated on one of the hairpin bends is ☀ *Casa degli Spiriti* which was awarded a Michelin star in 2011 and where the food is the best money can buy *(Nov–Feb closed Mon–Thu | on the road from Costermano to San Zeno di Montagna | tel. 04 56 20 07 66 | www.casadeglispiriti.it | Expensive).* INSIDER TIP Fantastic view of the lake from the dining room and terrace. San Zeno is not the small modest village tucked far away in the mountains, as you might expect, but is a winter sports resort. Accommodation e. g. in *Hotel Sole (Via*

Cá Schena 1 | tel. 04 57 28 50 01 | www. albergosole.com | Budget), dining in *Albergo Ristorante Al Cacciatore (closed Mon | Prada Bassa | tel. 04 57 28 51 39 | Budget).*

LAZISE

(134 C4) (∅ H7) The little village seems almost seems as if it wants to ward off visitors: the 14th-century fortified walls around the Old Town of Lazise (pop. 1000) are still fully intact, and you can only enter through three gateways.

It is significantly quieter here than in any of the other places on the east shore and this makes the pretty old place with its unusually large *piazza* all the more attractive. Lazise was an important trading post when under Venetian rule. A visible reminder of that time can be seen in the customs house at the harbour, from where Venice kept a watch on the trading of goods on the lake.

SIGHTSEEING

SAN NICOLÒ
The 12th-century church is right on the harbourside. It has since been secularised and was used at some time as a theatre. The delightful frescos have been restored and are now on view once again.

SCALIGER CASTLE
The castle dates from the 12th and 13th centuries and can only be viewed from the outside, as it is a private residence. Scaliger Castle was fortified to protect Lazise harbour.

TOWN WALL
The fact that a wall was built around almost all of the Old Town of Lazise has an historical explanation: Venice continually

If staying at Locanda San Vigilio is too expensive, you can still treat yourself to a drink

strengthened its outposts on Lake Garda against attacks from Milan.

over the lake, there are also seven wonderfully comfortable rooms. *Daily | Via*

Lazise's little harbour was once an important trading centre under Venetian rule

FOOD & DRINK

AL CASTELLO

Sitting in a large inner courtyard, right next to the town wall, guests can enjoy grilled trout, spaghetti with clams and other specialities, served by efficient and friendly waiters. *Closed Thu | Via Porta del Lion 8 | tel. 04 56 47 10 22 | Moderate*

CLASSIQUE ●

One of the most beautifully situated restaurants on the lake in an historical villa located slightly above the lakeside promenade. You'll find the view across the lake quite breath-taking. Inside, you can marvel at the floor mosaics. And for those who want to wake up to a view

Albarello 33 | tel. 04 57 58 02 70 | www. ristoclassique.it | Moderate

CORTE OLIVO

Pizza and co. can be enjoyed here in one of the most beautiful courtyards just inside the town walls. *Closed Mon | Corso Cangrande 22 | tel. 04 57 58 13 47 | Moderate*

LA FORGIA

The former smithy is now a fish restaurant where the chef de cuisine, Omero Rossignoli, has specialised in all types of seafood – grilled, of course. After all, an open fire is always to be found in a forge. *Closed Mon | Via Calle 1 | tel. 04 57 58 02 87 | www.ristorantelaforgia.it | Expensive*

GIPI'S BAR

For colour-coded relaxation, be sure to order an aperitif in this bar to match the sunsets, such as an orange mixture of Aperol, sparkling white wine and mineral water. *Daily | Via F. Fontana 16*

SHOPPING

INSIDER TIP L'ARTE DEL BERE

'The Art of Drinking' is the name of this *enoteca*, based on the notion that life is too short to drink poor wine. The extensive list of wines proves how appropriate the name is. *Via Cansignorio 10*

MARKET

A market is held every Wed morning on Lungolago Marconi.

LEISURE, SPORT & BEACH

A small strip of sand follows the shoreline south of the village. Guided bicycle tours can be booked through the large bike shop *Los Locos (Via Gardesana 71 | tel. 04 57 58 13 49 | www.loslocosbikeshop.com)* which, apart from mountain bikes, also has other types of bike to rent that are more difficult to find – namely INSIDER TIP racing bikes.

ENTERTAINMENT

The evenings in Lazise are a quiet affair. Just sit on the large *Piazza Vittorio Emanuele* and enjoy a glass of wine.

WHERE TO STAY

CANGRANDE GARNI

Guests staying in this elegant *palazzo* next to the medieval walls around Lazise can soak up the peace and quiet. The Girasole winebar is in the same building. *23 rooms | Corso Cangrande 16 | tel. 04 56 47 04 10 | www.cangrandehotel.it | Moderate*

IL GIARDINO DEGLI ULIVI

All rooms in this *agriturismo* guesthouse have lovely views of the lake. There is also a small pool and you can buy olive oil directly from the producer here too. *6 rooms | Via Fossalta 12 | tel. 04 56 47 10 38 | www.ilgiardinodegliulivi.info | Budget–Moderate*

ALLA GROTTA

The location of this little guesthouse right next to the small harbour is delightful. Gourmets come to Alla Grotta for its wonderful fish dishes but you can also stay here too, less exclusively than you would expect when looking at the menu. *12 rooms | Via Fontana 5 | tel. 04 57 58 00 35 | www.allagrotta.it | Budget–Moderate*

PIANI DI CLODIA

This four-star campsite with three pools also has several flats to rent and pitches for motor homes and caravans. *Via Fossalta 42 | tel. 04 57 59 04 56 | www.pianidiclodia.it*

AGRITURISMO LE TESE

This peacefully situated property, surrounded by vineyards – mostly Bardolino – is particularly welcoming. Homemade cake is served for breakfast. *3 flats | Colà di Lazise | tel. 04 57 59 53 14 | www.letese.it | Moderate*

INFORMATION

Via Fontana 14 | tel. 04 57 58 01 14 | www.comune.lazise.vr.it

OUTINGS

BORGHETTO DI VALEGGIO SUL MINCIO (0) (*𝄞 0*)

A good 30-min drive along the Mincio will lead you to Borghetto di Valeggio sul Mincio. Just before reaching the village,

LAZISE

you pass over a INSIDER TIP gigantic stone bridge that was designed as a dam. Giangaleazzo Visconti, a ruler from Milan, dammed the Mincio back in 1393. The river was used to fill a moat around Mantua that was under Venetian rule. If the water were not there, they feared that the town would be easy to take. It took just eight months to complete the dam that is 600 m (1968 ft) long, 26 m (85 ft) wide and 10 m (33 ft) high.

Bursting with flowers and a green idyll: Parco Giardino Sigurtà

Antica Locanda Mincio (closed Wed/Thu | Via Buonarroti 12 | tel. 04 57 95 00 59 | www.anticalocandamincio.it | Expensive) is one of the best restaurants in the region (reservation essential!). Top-quality cooking can also be enjoyed in the *Bottega Osteria Al Ponte (closed Wed | Via Buonarroti 24 | tel. 04 56 37 00 74 | www. bottegaosteriaalponte.com | Moderate–Expensive).* Originally just a room at the back of the grocery shop, the local produce and its preparation by the Cressoni family became so popular that an *osteria* was opened.

PARCO GIARDINO SIGURTÀ
(0) (*m O*)
The 124-acre gardens and park 14 km (8½ mi) to the south can be explored on foot, by bike or aboard a little train – failing that you can rent an electrically driven tricycle. *Open mid March–mid Nov, daily 9am–7pm | (March, Oct, Nov until 6pm) | www.sigurta.it*

TERMALE DEL GARDA ●
(134 C5) (*m H7*)
Hot water bubbles out of the ground further inland. You can bathe in the waters in the hot-spring baths in *Colà di Lazise*, which have a temperature of 37°C and are open until late. Concerts are held in the evenings in the park with its ancient trees and in the Villa dei Cedri. *Tel. 04 57 59 09 88 | www.parcotermaledelgarda.it*

PESCHIERA DEL GARDA
(134 C5) (*m H8*)
Peschiera is a further 8 km (5 mi) to the south at the southern-most point of Lake Garda. This is where the water from the lake, fed by the Sarca in Riva in the north, flows out as the Mincio in the south towards the Po and ultimately into the Adriatic Sea. The Mincio forms the boundary between the regions of Veneto and

Lombardy. From 1516 onwards, Peschiera came under the rule of Venice. The Austro-Venetian fortresses are particularly worth visiting. A lot of trains on the Milan–Venice route stop at Peschiera.

The history of fishing on Lake Garda can be traced in the *Museo della Pesca e della Tradizione | Thu 5pm–6pm | www.amici delgondolin.it)* in the former Habsburg barracks on the left-hand side of the Canale di Mezzo. It includes photographs, fishing equipment and information on the geology of the lake.

Anyone who fancies a day away from the lake and a gentle bike ride can follow the course of the Muncio from Peschiera to Mantova – which is flat all the way. Almost 40 km (25 mi) along a cycle path. For the return journey you can even take the train. If you don't have your own bike with you, you can rent one from *Motocicli Ardielli (Via Venezia 66 | tel. 04 57 55 01 24).*

A stroll around the narrow streets in the Old Town is also a delight. If you want to soak up its tranquillity head for the *Gelateria Centrale (Via Dante 21)* and take a table overlooking the Mincio canal. 'From the field to the table' is the motto of the ☺ *market (Thu mornings | Piazza F. di Savoia)* where local farmers sell their seasonal produce: fresh, from just around the corner, sold directly to the customer – fair trade on an everyday scale!

Accommodation is available in *Bell'Arrivo (27 rooms | Piazzetta Benacense 2 | tel. 04 56 40 13 22 | www.hotelbellarrivo. it | Budget–Moderate).* Good food (with eel as a speciality) can be found at *La Torretta (closed Wed | Via Galilei 12 | tel. 04 57 55 01 08 | Moderate).* The small INSIDER TIP *Osteria Goto* on the edge of the Old Town can be recommended *(closed Thu | tel. 04 57 55 01 08 | Moderate).* The young chefs produce excellent pasta dishes – and it has become a popular place to eat among young locals.

VERONA ● (135 F5) (*Ø K8*)

Whoever has had enough of the holiday atmosphere and lying on beaches, and who fancies a bit of city life, should head off for Verona. The city, just 25 km (15½ mi) to the east (pop. 264,000) has a whole range of sites of immense cultural importance as well as a pedestrian precinct where you can shop till you drop. But before you leap in your car and set off for Verona – how about taking the train? From the south of the lake this is no problem at all – and from many other towns on Lake Garda there is a regular bus service to Verona. The *Verona Card* is a combined ticket for entrance to museums, churches and major sites of interest as well as for travelling on public transport within the city of Verona; a one-day ticket costs 8 euros (available in every museum).

Due to its position at the end of the route that crosses the Alps via the lowest mountain pass, the Brenner, Verona developed into an important city under the Romans. And Verona's most famous structure dates from Roman times: the ★ *Arena di Verona (Mon 1.30pm–7.30 pm, Tue–Sun 9am–7pm | on days operas are performed 9am–3.30pm | Piazza Bra | ticket office: Via Dietro Anfiteatro 6b | tel. 04 58 00 51 51 | www.arena.it).* Start your tour of the city from here. The Roman amphitheatre,

---

CITY WHERE TO START?
Piazza Bra: The large square where the arena is, makes the perfect starting point for a tour of the city. It's best to arrive by train and it's only a ten-minute walk from Porta Nuova station to the city centre. If you prefer to travel by car, there is a multi-storey car park on Piazza Citadella close to the arena.

If you don't want to go to the opera, you can still visit the arena in Verona during the day

dating from the 1st century AD, was badly damaged by an earthquake in the 12th century. Only four arches which were part of the outer wall are still standing today. The Arena can be visited during the day, but it is best seen in its full glory on one of its famous opera evenings. The première of these performances was Verdi's Aida to commemorate the composer's 100 birthday in August 1913.

The Via Roma from the Arena will take you to the *Castelvecchio (Tue until Sun 8.30am–7.30pm, Mon 1.45pm–7.30pm).* The brick-red castle of 1534 is the largest building erected under the Scaligers. Temporary exhibitions are held within its walls. Walking upriver along the upper bank next to the Adige you will reach the Piazza Portichetti. This is a slight detour, but it leads to San Zeno Maggiore – the church best loved by the locals – with its stunning portal decorated with 48 bronze panels. Detailed information on Verona's

churches can be found under *www.chiese verona.it.*

Now take the same route back to the arena. Fancy a refreshing drink in the main square? Drop in at the Piazza Bra in *Via Mazzini*, Verona's main shopping street. This leads to the *Piazza delle Erbe*, where a fruit and vegetable market is held every day in the former Roman forum.

Our tour continues via the *Piazza dei Signori* and the *Scavi Scaligeri* where photography exhibitions, organised by the Centro Internazionale di Fotografia, are regularly held in the excavated areas. The *Scaliger tombs* are nearby: above the Gothic graves of the former ruling dynasty are life-sized equestrian statues of family members.

At *Via Cappello 23* close by, there is an unremarkable 14th-century house that virtually ever visitor to Verona has to have seen – whether or not they have ever read Shakespeare's famous *Romeo and Juliet* or not. Casa Capuleti is the official name of Juliet's house *(Mon 1.30pm–7.30pm, Tue–Sun 8.30am–7.30pm)*. Touching the right-hand breast of the statue of Juliet in the inner courtyard is supposed to bring good luck! The lovers' balcony – which appears on virtually every postcard of Verona – was, however, only added to the façade in 1940.

The INSIDER TIP *Osteria Sgarzarie (closed Mon | Corte Sgarzarie 14a | tel. 04 58 00 03 12 | www.sgarzarie.it | Moderate)* not far from the Piazza Erbe, is a good place to eat, far from the madding crowd. Veronese cuisine can be enjoyed in the *Trattoria Tre Marchetti (closed Mon lunchtime and all day Sun, closed Mon only in July/Aug | Vicolo Tre Marchetti 19b | tel. 04 58 03 04 63 | www.tremarchetti.it | Expensive)*. The restaurant is one of the best the city has to offer and has received numerous awards. For those staying the night, the *Locanda Catullo (21 rooms | Via Valerio Catullo 1 | tel. 04 58 00 27 86 | locandacatullo@tiscalinet.it | Budget)* is a cosy place in the heart of the city. Information: *Piazza Bra | tel. 04 58 06 86 80; Piazza XXV Aprile | tel. 04 58 00 08 61 | www.tourism.verona.it*

TORRI DEL BENACO

(134 C2) *(⌀ H6)* **The best way to get to Torri del Benaco (pop. 2900) is to take the ferry from Maderno. It is a very practical way to travel – unless one wants to drive half way round the lake to visit the opposite shore.**

From the lake it is clear to see how Scaliger Castle guards the town. Or 'guarded', to be more precise – as today you can walk right in: its walls now being home to a folk museum. In 1383 the Scaliger ruler Antonio della Scala, had the fortress, which dates from the 9th century, turned into a residence. During renovation work in the 20th century a pink coloured marble plaque was discovered in the castle, which bears a carved relief of the Scaliger coat-of-arms – a 'scale' in the form of a ladder with five rungs, now on show in the museum.

Torri del Benaco is one of the quieter places on the east shore and is not nearly as overrun as its neighbours Garda or even Bardolino. The oval-shaped harbour stretches right into the town itself and provides shelter to rows of little fishing boats, all strung out in a line like pearls on a thread. There are just a few narrow lanes that lead away from the harbour basin and there is often surprising little going on. The countryside beyond Torri del Benaco is not as steep as elsewhere, Monte Baldo is slightly further away here from the lake which makes the place that much more open.

SIGHTSEEING

MUSEO DEL CASTELLO SCALIGERO ●

In the folk museum in Scaliger Castle a good insight can be gained of how the people on Lake Garda used to live before the tourists came, earning their living primarily from fishing and the olive industry. The displays on boat building and the rock engravings in the area are particularly interesting. Visitors to the museum can also see a INSIDER TIP lemon glasshouse built in 1760 – the only one on the east shore that is still being used. Legend has it that the art of lemon growing was first brought to Lake Garda by Franciscan monks. *June–Sept Tue–Sun 9.30am–1pm and 4.30pm–7.30pm, April/May and Oct 9.30am–12.30pm and 2.30pm–6pm | Viale Fratelli Lavanda 2 | www.museodel castelloditorridelbenaco.it*

TORRI DEL BENACO

SANTI PIETRO E PAOLO
The large church organ of 1744, which is still used, is an unusual one to find in Italy. Another unusual feature in this Baroque church is the bronze statue of the sometime priest, Giuseppe Nascimbeni, who was beatified in 1988. Nascimbeni founded the charitable convent in Torri.

SANTISSIMA TRINITÀ
Beautifully renovated frescos by the School of Giotto can be admired in the little church by the harbour, tucked away in the corner of the Piazza Calderini.

FOOD & DRINK

ALLA GROTTA
Red canvas chairs welcome guests to the small wooden terrace above the lake. And what's on the menu? Seafood. *Closed Mon | Corso Dante Alighieri 57 | tel. 04 57 22 58 39 | Moderate*

TRATTORIA LONCRINO
Only 500 m from the centre, in Loncrino, you can tuck into local food served in a relaxed atmosphere, sample the wines recommended and enjoy a view of the lake from the terrace. *Closed Tue | Loncrino 10 | tel. 04 56 29 00 18 | Budget–Moderate*

RISTORANTE VIOLA
A restaurant with an unusual history. Over a period of several years, the chef-de-cuisine Isidoro Consolini succeeded in developing Al Caval – as this restaurant used to be called – into a gourmet's paradise. Consolini met the famous Spanish star chef Ferran Adrià and introduced molecular gastronomy to Lake Garda and was soon awarded his first Michelin star. The only problem was that the people around Lake Garda didn't really appreciate this elevated cuisine. So they remodelled the restaurant and gave it the name of Consolini's wife. The star disappeared but, for all that you can now eat extremely well and less expensively than before. *Closed Wed and at lunchtimes except on Sun | Via Gardesana 186 | tel. 04 57 22 50 83 | www ristoranteviola.com | Expensive*

SHOPPING

ANTIQUE MARKET
In the summer months an antique market is held in the Old Town from 8pm–midnight

BELL'ARTE
This art gallery has been running for years now. And apart from more usual still-lifes and large oil paintings, it also has something unusual in its portfolio: large-format pictures of motifs taken from Antiquity, worked in the manner of historical fresco paintings, which are produced by restorers from Florence. *Via Dante Alighieri 94 | www. galleria-bell-arte-torridelbenaco-marika-hilmar.com*

MARKET
Every Monday morning a market is held on the road along the shore.

LEISURE, SPORT & BEACH

A long beach (free access) can be found at the southern end of the village; a few willow trees offer a little shade. 'Tra gli Olivi i Tesori di Torri del Benaco', 'Between the olive trees, the treasures of Torri' is the name of a path that will take you to nine little churches in the area. A brochure is available from the tourist information office. Plan a whole day for this outing.

ENTERTAINMENT

In summer an open-air cinema is held in the castle walls.

An old *palazzo* right on the harbour with deliciously prepared fresh fish: Albergo Gardesana

WHERE TO STAY

GARDESANA

There is no more beautiful place to stay in Torri than here – that's if you can do without a pool. As a reward you sleep in the Palazzo dei Capitani, originally built as the town-hall, directly on the harbourside. *34 rooms | Piazza Calderini 20 | tel. 04 57 22 54 11 | www.hotel-gardesana. com | Expensive*

AI SALICI

Although this no-frills campsite is on the other side of the road from the lake, there is a tunnel leading to the beach. *Via Pai di Sotto 97 | tel. 04 57 26 01 96 | www. gardalake.it/aisalici*

VILLA SUSY

The small hotel is just a few minutes walk from the heart of the Old Town, down on the lake. Nice beach, the rooms overlooking the lake are lovely – on the other side the traffic streams along the Gardesana.

14 rooms | Via Gardesana 119 | tel. 04 57 22 59 65 | www.villasusy.com | Moderate

INFORMATION

Viale Fratelli Lavanda 2 | tel. 04 57 22 51 20 | www.torridelbenaco.de

OUTINGS

ALBISANO ☙ (134 C2) (⌀ H6)

'Garda's balcony' is how the Italian poet Gabriele D'Annunzio described Albisano, 2 km (1¼ mi) up from Torri del Benaco, clinging onto the ridge of Monte Baldo. Holiday-makers who like to do things in comfort, can drive up here, but whoever wants to earn such a magical view should go on foot. The footpath is waymarked just after the turning to Albisano. The short hike will take you 45 minutes – and is pretty steep. But then you'll be gasping for breath anyway when you get to the top – the INSIDER TIP view from the terrace of Albisano parish church is breathtakingly beautiful.

SOUTH SHORE

Two extremes meet at the south of Lake Garda: on the one hand there is the little town of Desenzano, a lively place full of people. Sirmione, however, is quite the opposite. It is really just a small village and, while its narrow streets may sound to the voices of the many tourists who visit during the day, in the evening it is particularly quiet.

The south shore of Lake Garda is embedded in a landscape that has little in common with that at the northern end of the lake. Desenzano lies in a wide bay. Sirmione is inimitably romantic: located on a long, narrow peninsula, it juts right out into the waters of the lake. The Old Town with its maze of lanes is one of the lake's tourist

hot spots. Just as the south of Lake Garda draws the visitor today, in the past it was bitterly fought over. In 1859 blood flowed on the battlefields of Solferino, when Italy fought against Austria in the Second Italian War of Independence.

DESENZANO

(133 D5) (*∅ F7*) ● While other towns may have nicer lakeside promenades, Desenzano's harbour wall is hard to beat. It comes as no surprise that it is not just the fishermen who can be found here when the sun goes down – this romantic spot is a favourite among couples, too.

Photo: Sirmione Castle

Roman remains, shops and nightlife: in Desenzano and Sirmione you'll find yourself immersed in the Italian way of life

Desenzano, with a population of more than 26,000, is the largest town on Lake Garda – and, to be more precise, the oldest. When the glaciers started to retreat northwards at the end of the last Ice Age that carved out the basin of Lake Garda, this was the first area around the lake that could support life. The Romans later settled here as the excavation of a villa with beautiful floor mosaics from the 3rd century goes to prove. Desenzano was repeatedly the object of foreign rulers' desire as its harbour at the southern end of the lake was strategically important for trade.

What it lacks in the way of beaches it makes up for with its bustling street life. Good shops and window displays can be found in the extensive pedestrian precinct, and you can easily spend hours over a cappuccino or two in one of the cafés on the Piazza Matteotti just watching

DESENZANO

Like the whole town, the shore promenade in Desenzano is also very lively

the comings and goings. And in the evenings, it's very hard finding a place in any of the bars around the old harbour. On Friday and Saturday evenings, right up until midnight, the narrow pedestrianised streets are completely chock-a-block. Young people from all around meet up here, styled through and through and ready for a flirt. After strolling around they head off for the discos in the vicinity.

SIGHTSEEING

CASTELLO ☀
It is worth taking INSIDER TIP a short stroll to Desenzano Castle for the view, as there are few other possibilities to enjoy such as far-reaching vista of the surrounding countryside from anywhere else along the flat south shore. *April–Oct Tue until Sun 9.30am–noon and 3.30pm–6pm*

LUNGOLAGO CESARE BATTISTI
Walking along the lakeside promenade you have a lovely view across the water –

and of the motorboats that sometimes race past at an incredible speed. But they are nothing compared to what Francesco Agello did here back in 1934: he set up a new record by reaching a speed of 709 km/h (440 mph)! A sculpture in the Mayer & Splendid hotel commemorates this deed that has been interpreted in the fascist manner of the period.

MUSEO CIVICO ARCHEOLOGICO G. RAMBOTTI
The museum is housed in a 15th-century cloister – that alone is worth seeing. One of the most interesting exhibits is a 2-m-long oak plough dating from the 2nd century BC. *Tue–Sun 3pm–7pm, in the peak summer season Tue–Thu 4pm–8.30pm, Fri 5pm–9.30pm, Sat/Sun 5pm–8.30pm | Chiostro di Santa Maria de Senioribus | Via T. Dal Molin 7 c*

SANTA MARIA MADDALENA
The principal church in Desenzano is the work of the architect Giulio Todeschini. It contains paintings by Zenone Veronese

and Andrea Celesti, which are well worth seeing. *The Last Supper* by Giambattista Tiepolo (1696–1770) is rightfully famous. Piazza Malvezzi

VILLA ROMANA

The carpenter Emanuele Zamboni was probably less enthusiastic about history after he discovered the remains of a 100 m² (1100 sq. ft) Roman yeoman's dwelling when digging the foundations for a house he wanted to build on the site in 1921. The floor mosaics are especially interesting, as is the hypocaust, the Roman equivalent to today's under-floor heating. *Tue until Sun 8.30am–7pm (in winter until 5pm) | Via Crocefisso 22*

FOOD & DRINK

RESTAURANT LA CONTRADA

This elegant *osteria* furnished with antiques has an emphasis on Lombard and Venetian cuisine such as *risotto all'amarone* (a full-bodied red wine which you can also order) or *baccalá* (dried cod) *alla vicentina*. *Closed Wed | Via Bagatta 12 | tel. 03 09 14 25 14 | Expensive*

DE' CORTE POZZI

This *enoteca* has recently moved into the courtyard of a *palazzo*. And if you get hungry when sampling the wines, you can also eat here – such as grilled steak. *Daily | Via Stretta Castello 3 | tel. 03 09 14 19 80 | Moderate*

KAPPERI

More like a place in a city – stylish and loud – that's what they love in Desenzano. Choice food is served in the spacious restaurant area and in the pretty garden. But there are also pizzas that attract a younger crowd. *Closed Tue | Via Nazario Sauro 7 | tel. 03 09 99 18 93 | www.kapperi. eu | Moderate–Expensive*

SQUARE 16

There is a good view of the moorings from the first floor of this chic eatery. The ground floor is the haunt of the younger crowd who sip their wine until 2am. *Closed Tue | Piazza Matteotti 16 | tel. 03 09 12 04 92 | Moderate–Expensive*

GELATERIA VIVALDI ☺

The ice cream here is the best in town – and only cream and milk from organic farms is used. *Piazza Matteotti 9*

VIVI

Large salads are a speciality of this modest restaurant – and the big pizzas are popular with the young. *Closed Tue | Piazza Matteotti 15 | tel. 03 09 91 49 50 | Budget*

SHOPPING

FRANTOIO DI MONTECROCE

Fresh and (cold) pressed olive oil can be bought at this *azienda agricola* in Montecroce. *Viale E. Andreis 84 | www.frantoiomontecroce.it*

★ **Grotte di Catullo**
In Sirmione: not caves but the remains of a Roman villa with a view of the lake → p. 76

★ **Rocca Scaligera Sirmione**
A moated castle, built on Roman foundations, rises out the lake like in a fairy tale → p. 77

★ **Lido delle Bionde**
A large pebbly beach in Sirmione with a café and paddle-boats, where the water is not deep → p. 78

MARCO POLO HIGHLIGHTS

IL LEONE DI LONATO

120 shops can be found in this shopping centre 2 km (1¼ mi) from the Desenzano motorway exit in the direction of Castiglione delle Stiviere. *Tue–Sun 9am–10pm, Mon 1pm–10pm | www.illeonedilonato.com*

LIBRERIA CASTELLI PODAVINI

When you run out of things to read on holiday, head for this place. The owner does not just stock the usual who-dunnits and good beach reads but also a broad selection of literature. And you don't just have to be fluent in Italian. You'll enjoy browsing here for English titles and looking at all the art and photography books, too. *Piazza Duomo 25*

MARKETS

Every first Sun of the month – except in August – an antiques market is held in the Old Town. The food market is every Tues morning on the road next to the lake.

LEISURE, SPORT & BEACHES

The *Lido di Padenghe* has a large pebbly and sandy beach and is free of charge; the *Lido di Lonato* also costs nothing and has very fine pebbles. The *Spiaggia Comunale*, a large pebbly beach, is to the north of Desenzano. Between Desenzano and the Sirmione peninsula, as well as to the north along the hilly Valtenesi, you will come across a number of other places to swim or sunbathe. A brochure is available from the tourist information office with recommended **INSIDER TIP** GPS cycling tours *(Itinerari con il GPS)*. These can also be downloaded under *www.comune. desenzano.brescia.it/italian/itinerari_bici. php*. Bikes can be hired from *Bikes Girelli (Via Annunciata 10 | tel. 03 09 11 97 97)*. Divers can head for the *Asso Sub Il Pellicano* diving centre *(Via Castello 1 | tel. 03 09 14 44 49)*.

ENTERTAINMENT

For those infected by Saturday-night-fever there's no avoiding Desenzano – the town is *the* nightlife centre on the lake.

GELATERIA CRISTALLO

A popular bar in the evening – perhaps because of the swing seats, from which you get a good view of the nightlife around the old harbour. *Via Porto Vecchio 12*

DEHOR

An exclusive address that has evolved out of the legendary Genux, formerly Italy's largest disco. *Open on Tue, Fri and Sat. Turn right 2 km (1¼ mi) from the Desenzano motorway exit in the direction of Castiglione delle Stiviere | www.dehordiscoteca.alter vista.org*

WHERE TO STAY

CAMPING

Desenzano has three campsite: the holiday village *Vo' (Via Vo' 4–9 | tel. 03 09 12 13 25 | www.voit.it)*, San Francesco *(Strada Vicinale San Francesco | tel. 03 09 11 02 45 | www. campingsanfrancesco.com)* and Italia *(Via Zamboni | tel. 03 09 11 02 77)*. Numerous other sites can be found in Valtenesi between Desenzano and Salò. Further information available from the tourist office in *San Felice del Benaco (Piazza Municipio 1 | tel. 0 36 56 25 41)*.

MAYER & SPLENDID

The erstwhile noble hotel is situated right on the promenade (unfortunately a busy through road). The plaster may be cracking on the ceiling but where else, at such a price, can you wake up and see the glittering water through French windows? *57 rooms | Piazza Ulisse Papa | tel. 03 09 14 22 53 | www.hotelmayeresplendid. com | Moderate*

HOTEL NAZIONALE
This hotel was once one of the oldest in Desenzano; now it is the most modern. A cool, restrained, no-frills design. *41 rooms / Via Marconi 23 / tel. 03 09 15 85 55 / www. nazionaleonline.it / Moderate–Expensive*

HOTEL PICCOLA VELA
Located in a park surrounded by olive trees this hotel is a special favourite thanks to its friendly staff. There is also a pool in the garden. *40 rooms / Via T. dal Molin 36 / tel. 03 09 91 46 66 / www.piccolavela.it / Moderate*

PIROSCAFO
This small hotel has been in the same family for generations. Located right next to the old harbour in the heart of the Old Town. *32 rooms / Via Porto Vecchio 11 / tel. 03 09 14 11 28 / www.hotelpiroscafo.it / Moderate*

INFORMATION
Via Porto Vecchio 34 / tel. 03 09 14 15 10 / www.provincia.brescia.it/turismo

OUTINGS

SOLFERINO AND SAN MARTINO DELLA BATTAGLIA (133 E6) (Ⓜ G8)
The area around Lake Garda was frequently the scene of fierce battles. Among the bloodiest were the Battle of San Martino della Battaglia and the Battle of Solferino. Both villages are just south of Desenzano. In 1859, the Italian Risorgimento, fighting for the unification of Italy, defeated the Austrian army under Emperor Franz Joseph. The foundations for a united Italy were laid. The unification of Italy included the Venetian Republic annexed from Austria, Piedmont ruled by the House of Savoy, the Kingdom of Sicily and papal Rome – and could only be achieved at the cost of 25,000 lives. And then there were tens of thousands of wounded left on the battle-fields to their own fate. This made the name Solferino known throughout the world. Henri Dunant, an extremely rich Swiss man, was so shocked at the sight of these soldiers who nobody was helping

It looks pretty harmless today, but it caused a lot of heartache: a canon in Solferino museum

that he founded the Red Cross – originally a charitable organisation set up to aid the wounded.

7000 skulls have been preserved in the church of *San Pietro* in Solferino as a reminder of the atrocities of war. *San Martino* also has a tower, erected as a monument, 74 m (243 ft) high. Inside, a series of frescoes relates to the history of the Risorgimento. *www.solferinoesan martino.it*

SIRMIONE

MAP INSIDE BACK COVER
(133 E6) *(🗺 G7)*
The town (pop. 8000) has a stunning location: the prominent peninsula juts out right in the middle of the south shore and points northwards.

Sirmione is one of the best-known towns on Lake Garda, with countless day trippers adding to the number of other holiday-makers staying here, including spa guests. It's hardly surprising that the pretty streets in the Old Town often get hopelessly crowded. The historical centre beyond the footbridge near the Scaliger castle can be visited only on foot – and due to the wide canal dug around the castle, the Old Town was turned into an island. Sirmione has not just attracted tourists in modern times. In Roman days its thermal spa was well known. The hot sulphurous spring water, at almost 70°C (158°F), emerges from below the bed of the lake, 300 m (985 ft) north-east of the 4 km-long (2½ mi) peninsula.

SIGHTSEEING

GROTTE DI CATULLO ★ ●
Catullus was right: he could hardly have chosen a more beautiful spot on Lake Garda. However, the representative villa, known as the Grotte di Catullo, was definitely not built by him as he was not wealthy enough.

But what does it matter whether the Roman poet Catullus ever lived on this spot at the south of the lake. It is a delightful location where he probably wrote his eulogy: "O beautiful Sirmione, the gem of all peninsulas and islands." An excursion to this impressive site is more than worthwhile: you can take a walk through olive groves and look at the extensive remains of the walls. The entrance fee includes a visit to the INSIDER TIP ▶ *archeological mu-*

The Piazza Carducci where the boats come in is a popular place for people to meet in Sirmione

seum. The clearly labelled displays provide a good overview of the whole site as well as of the early history of Lake Garda. *Tue–Sat 8.30am–7pm (in winter until 5pm), Sun 9am–6pm (in winter until 2pm).*

ROCCA SCALIGERA ★ ●

In the 13th century, Mastino della Scala had a moated castle built inside the protective walls on top of the Roman foundations. Occasionally exhibitions are held in the old fortress grounds at the entrance to the Old Town. But even without any cultural extras the castle has a lot on offer, such as its ☀ tower from where there is a lovely view over the rooftops of the Old Town. St Anna's, with its 17th-century Baroque interior, is a little 14th-century church in the castle boasting 15th-century frescos. If you fancy some refreshments: for years now, a wonderful old fruit stand has been in place outside the castle, selling pieces of melon and quartered pineapples, slices of lemon and coconut boats.

April–Oct Tue–Sun 8.30am–7.30pm, Nov–March 9am–1pm

SAN PIETRO IN MAVINO

The pretty Romanesque church was built in 765 by Lombardic monks on the remains of a heathen temple It is located a little off the beaten track on the path to the Roman site. A fresco inside dating from 1321, depicting the Last Judgement, is well worth seeing.

FOOD & DRINK

AL PROGRESSO

A restaurant that has managed to survive despite the fast-food outlets in Sirmione's streets. The *bavette al salmerino* with vodka and flambéed *gamberoni* are specialities. In the summer season *lavarello* is served fresh from the lake. *Closed Thu | Via Vittorio Emanuele 18 | tel. 0 30 916 1 08 | Moderate–Expensive*

LA RUCOLA

The restaurant belongs to the association of 'Jeunes Restaurateurs d'Europe. INSIDER TIP ► The cuisine is light and sophisticated. The menu, changed on a monthly basis, has a Mediterranean slant. *Closed Fri lunchtime and Thu. | Vicolo Strentelle 3 | tel. 0 30 9163 26 | www.ristorantelarucola. it | Expensive*

LA SPERANZINA

Spicy spaghetti with peperoncino and red tuna tatare are among the specialities of this *antica trattoria*. You can enjoy your meal in the peaceful garden with a view of the lake. *Closed Mon Nov–March | Via Dante 16 | tel. 03 09 90 62 92 | www.lasp eranzina.it | Expensive*

OSTERIA AL TORCOL

This authentic wine tavern is just a hop, skip and jump from the main thoroughfare, the

The long jetty at Sirmione's Lido delle Bionde doubles as a sun-deck for the young

Via Vittorio Emanuele. Modest meals are also served, such as a vegetarian lasagne. *Closed Wed | Via San Salvatore 30 | tel. 03 09 90 46 05 | Moderate–Expensive*

SHOPPING

The narrow streets of the Old Town on the peninsula are bursting with a huge variety of shops.

MARKET
There is no weekly market in the Old Town, but one in *Colombare (Mon)* and in *Lugana di Sirmione (Fri).*

OUTLET
In Italy virtually every third shop is called an 'outlet' nowadays, but this one really is one: top-of-the-range Italian designer clothes can be found here at greatly reduced prices. They are still anything but cheap, but considerably less expensive than the regular price. *Via Vittorio Emanuele 74*

LEISURE, SPORT & BEACHES

Several free pebbly beaches are located on the south shore towards Peschiera. The *Grotte di Catullo* is a treeless beach, free of charge, situated below the excavation site. Unfortunately it can be reached only by paddle boat or yacht. The ★ ● *Lido delle Bionde* is a large flat pebbly beach at the north-east end of the peninsula. There is a café and paddle-boat hire, sunbeds and umbrellas rather like at a classic Mediterranean resort, complete with a long wooden jetty which doubles as a sunbathing deck and catwalk for the young and beautiful. Another beach that does not cost anything is near Scaliger Castle.
Hot water straight from the source is fed directly into the two public spa baths and

to the spa hotels. All spa facilities belong to the *Terme e Grandi Alberghi* group *(www.termedisirmione.com)*. The new spa centre, ● Aquario, is open to the general public *(March–Dec | Via Staffalo)* as is the *Stabilimento Termale* Virgilio *(March–Nov | Via Alfieri)*. Windsurfing, sailing and kajak school and hire centre: *Centro Surf Sirmione (Via Brescia 31 | tel. 03 09 19 61 30 | www.centrosurfsirmione.it)*; surfing school: *Martini (Lido Porto Galeazzi | tel. 0 30 91 62 08)*; waterskiing school and boat rental: *Bisoli (Via XXV Aprile 29 | tel. 0 30 91 60 88 | www.bisoli.com)*

WHERE TO STAY

THE GARDA VILLAGE

A comfortable and attractive campsite on the lake with its own private beach. *Colombare | Via Coorti Romane 47 | tel. 03 09 90 45 52 | www.gardavillage.it*

GRIFONE

All rooms have a beautiful view of the lake despite being a small hotel in the narrow streets of the historical Old Town – and it is surprisingly cheap, too. *16 rooms | Via Bocchio 4 | tel. 0 30 91 60 14 | grifone sirmione@gmail.com | Budget*

DEGLI OLEANDRI

Just stepping into the lobby tells you that this hotel is family run. Oil paintings hang on the walls of the staircase and carefully chosen antiques give the place an atmosphere of its own. *24 rooms | Via Dante 31 | tel. 03 09 90 57 80 | www.hoteldeglioleandri.it | Moderate*

PACE

From the hotel windows there is a wonderful view over the lake and the changing light at different times of day. *22 rooms | Piazza Porto Valentino 5 | tel. 03 09 90 58 77 | www.pacesirmione.it | Moderate*

CAMPING SIRMIONE

This three-star campsite with its own beach is closest to the Old Town. *Colombare | Via Sirmioncino 9 | tel. 030 91 90 45 | www.camping-sirmione.it*

VILLA CORTINE PALACE HOTEL

One of Sirmione's most elegant hotels set in lovely parklike grounds. An ugly extension has now spoilt the old villa. *55 rooms | Via Grotte 6 | tel. 03 09 90 58 90 | www.palacehotelvillacortine.it | Expensive*

INSIDER TIP ▶ VILLA PIOPPI

An old villa on the lake, only a 15 minute walk from the Old Town. Very basic but charming and in a beautiful location. *7 rooms | Via XXV Aprile 76 | tel. 03 09 90 41 19 | Budget*

INFORMATION

Viale Marconi 2 | Tel. 0 30 91 61 14 | www.sirmionehotel.com

LOW BUDGET

▶ Places for lunch can by found outside the Old Towns of Sirmione and Desenzano, especially on main roads, offering *pranzo al lavoro* – usually a three-course meal for 10 euros. Plain, very Italian and filling – a 'meal for workers' in fact.

▶ The normal end-of-season sale still exists in Italy – *saldi* is the magic word to look out for. Sales start in summer on the first Saturday in July; in winter around 7 Jan. In some shops, prices are halved – and shopping the Friday before will make you pretty annoyed. Sometimes there are even reductions of up to 70 percent.

WEST SHORE

And how did it all begin? In 1880 the German Louis Wimmer travelled down the west side of Lake Garda and recognised how much his fellow countrymen would like it. He began by building the Grand Hotel Gardone and, as such, set the stone rolling for tourism on Lake Garda. In the early 20th century, ever more luxury hotels went up, and instead of lemon trees, vineyards and olive groves, beautiful parks were laid out, whose old trees from those days still give this region its special charm. In 1921 the Italian poet Gabriele D'Annunzio, an eccentric and a dandy, came to live here. His house, Vittoriale degli Italiani, is now a museum and still retains the spirit of that time. That spirit, however, was soon to turn into a phantom – in 1943 Benito Mussolini declared the Facist *Repubblica Sociale Italiana* while in neighbouring Salò. Mussolino was living with his family at the Villa Feltrinelli in Gargnano, and he had arranged for his lover, Claretta Petacci, to stay in the Villa Fiordaliso, also in Gardone, which today is a first-class restaurant.

At the southern end of the west shore the mountains have taken a step back from the lake. There are no more tunnels here and the lakeside road winds its way elegantly along the shore-line or turns inland so that the old fishing villages huddled around their harbours, that form the commune of Gargnano, remain undisturbed.

Photo: Salò

The quieter corner of the lake favoured by the Italians: luxury living and gourmet dining on the west shore

Whoever comes here on holiday is not looking for an extreme sports adventure as in the north, nor for the family-friendly beaches along the east shore. Instead, visitors are more likely to be looking for a good cappuccino next to the lake – which at this point is so wide it can seem like the open sea when the weather is hazy. In the evening, the holiday-maker here likes to go out to eat, for this is where the best dining can be had.

GARDONE RIVIERA

(133 D–E2) *(ₘ F–G 5–6)* Even in the high season, the cafés here are never over-flowing. A table can always be found after a gentle stroll along the Lungolago – this is where the more leisurely tastes are well catered for.

GARDONE RIVIERA

The best thing about Gardone are its parks and gardens. Taking the steep roads and paths that lead up from the shore, you will find yourself walking in the shade of old cypress trees and magnolias. The gardens, along with the stately villas and old hotels, are testimony to Gardone's glorious past. A stay in Lungolago D'Annunzio can work wonders: here you can easily forget that the village is not even on the lakeside but above it. Gardone Sopra, with its houses all huddled around San Nicola's parish church, now has a population of 2700. This is where the roots of the village are to be found, although it has rather lost its importance today. A ☀ **INSIDER TIP** narrow path with a magnificent view of the lake winds its way between the houses. And everyone heads for *the* attraction *par excellence*, Vittoriale degli Italiani, the poet Gabriele D'Annunzio's retirement home.

Bizarre detail in Vittoriale: the bow of the warship 'Puglia'

SIGHTSEEING

GIARDINO BOTANICO HRUSKA ★ ●

Originally this botanic garden was just one of the many wonderful parks in the village, but since the Austrian artist and performer André Heller bought it at the end of the 1980s, it has become more than just that. Clanging fountains can be found among huge trees, and in one or other secret corner a modern sculpture by Keith Haring or Mimmo Paladino. André Heller enthuses about his collection of flora from different places from around the world, a paradise that he never ceases to wonder at: "Edelweiss in the middle of orchid meadows, ferns several feet high next to magnificent pomegranates. Streams and waterfalls with sacred koi, trout and reflections made by dragonflies, hills of dolomite rock next to cactii and towering ivies." *Daily March–Oct 9am–7pm | www.hellergarden.com*

MUSEO IL DIVINO INFANTE

Italian figures of the Christ Child over a period of 300 years make up the 200 pieces of this unique sculpture collection. *April–June and Sept Fri–Sun 10am–1pm and 3pm–7pm, July/Aug Tue–Sun 4pm–7pm, Dec–mid Jan Tue–Sun 10am–6pm | Via dei Colli 34 | www.il-bambino-gesu.com*

VITTORIALE DEGLI ITALIANI ★

A strange collection of buildings: this was where Gabriele D'Annunzio (1863–1938) had his last house built, in 1921, and is where he lived until his death. He left it to the State as a national monument. On view are the bow of the warship Puglia,

D'Annunzio's car and a plane from which the poet – who later was to support the Fascists – dropped leaflets over Vienna during World War I. There is an open-air theatre in the park where works by the author are performed in the summer. The upper part of the park is dominated by a Fascist mausoleum. The largest sarcophagus contains the mortal remains of the poet. Guided tours to the house are obligatory, whereas visitors are free to roam the park *(daily Oct–March 9am–5pm, April–Sept 8.30am–8pm)*. A war museum has been opened in part of the house and contains several items connected with D'Annunzio's wartime activities that, until now, have been kept in the repository *(April–Sept Tue–Sun 9.30am–7pm, Oct–March 9am–1pm and 2pm–5pm)*. *www.vittoriale.it*

Whether Enrico Pelligrini's creations really lend you wings in Agli Angeli?

FOOD & DRINK

AGLI ANGELI

Enrico Pellegrini's cooking in 'Among the Angels' is becoming more and more elegant and refined (pike hamburger with creamed beans). Reservations essential! A hotel of the same name with 16 rooms belongs to the *trattoria* which is in Gardone Sopra. *Closed Tue | Piazza Garibaldi 2 | tel. 0 36 52 09 91 | www.agliangeli.com | Moderate–Expensive*

★ **Giardino Botanico Hruska**
André Heller's dream garden on Lake Garda: modern sculptures are hidden in a magical park in Gardone Sopra
→ p. 82

★ **Vittoriale degli Italiani**
Gabriele D'Annunzio's residence in Gardone Riviera
→ p. 82

★ **Sant'Andrea Apostolo**
The church in Maderno with its pink, grey and white striped façade is unmistakable
→ p. 85

★ **Parco Fontanella**
One of the largest free beaches on the west shore in Gargnano → p. 87

★ **Terrazza del brivido**
The restaurant terraces in Pieve that jut out a long way above the lake → p. 90

★ **Lakeside in Salò**
Here you can do as the Romans do and promenade to your heart's content → p. 90

★ **Market in Salò**
In Salò you can buy almost anything → p. 93

MARCO POLO HIGHLIGHTS

BELVEDERE DA MARIETTA

Regional cooking; the pasta dishes are delicious, as is the whitefish. Plain food but tasty. The view out over the lake is unbeatable. And should it rain: the dining room is decorated in an equally pretty rustic style. *Closed Wed evening and all day Thu | Via Montecucco 78 | tel. 0 36 52 09 60 | Moderate*

INSIDER TIP ▶ SANS SOUCI

This charming eatery is in a vaulted cellar. The starters are especially good – such as the risotto with *radicchio* – but the crisp pizzas are well worth trying, too. *Closed Wed | Vicolo al Lago 12 | tel. 03 65 29 07 46 | Budget–Moderate*

SHOPPING

ANTIQUES MARKET

Small market every Sat from June to Sept 4pm–11pm on the lakeside promenade.

MARKET

Every Friday there is a market in the car-park at the Giardino Botanico.

LEISURE, SPORT & BEACHES

Spiaggia Rimbalzello to the south of the town costs 5 euros, incl. umbrella and sunbed. Free beaches are a rarity on this part of the lake: one is near the Villa delle Rose in Fasano and another, very small one can be found near the casino on Via Zanardelli.

ENTERTAINMENT

Gardone is better known for its culture than its nightlife. Live music can be enjoyed free of charge along the lake promenade on alternate evenings; in Vittoriale there are *theatre performances* and concerts. *Let the evening draw gently to a close over a drink in Caffè Wimmer (Piazza Wimmer 5)* or in Gardone Sopra in the *Bar Le Rose (Piazza Caduti 19)*. The *Bacco Poeta* is an inviting wine bar *(Piazza Caduti 22)*.

WHERE TO STAY

COLOMBER

This cosy, family-run hotel in San Michele in the mountains behind Gardone has been comprehensively renovated and now has a respectably sized pool in the garden – which is practical as the lake is quite a long way away. *18 rooms | Via Val di Sur 111 | tel. 0 36 52 11 08 | www.colomber.com | Budget–Moderate*

HOTEL DIANA

Plain rooms, but with balconies and a view of the lake – at a good price. *16 rooms | Lungolago Gabriele D'Annunzio 30 | tel. 0 36 52 18 15 | www.hoteldianagardone.it | Budget*

SAVOY PALACE

At long last someone has taken over this beautiful grand hotel that can look back at a 100-year-old history and many famous guests. Half of the complex is given over to flats, but part of it is still a hotel. The standard is high, the view fantastic as is the small pool. *60 rooms | Corso Zanardelli 2 | tel. 03 65 29 05 88 | www savoypalace.it | Expensive*

INSIDER TIP ▶ LE TRE GATTE

This B&B is in a quiet street. The owner's mother was English – and the furnishings have something of a British country house about them. *4 rooms | Vicolo Ars 10 | tel 03 65 29 04 40 | www.letregatte.com | Budget*

INFORMATION

Corso Repubblica 8 | tel. 0 36 52 03 47 www.rivieradeilimoni.it

OUTINGS

SAN MICHELE ☆ **(133 D2) (𝄞 F5)**

Whoever fancies a bit of exercise can take the hour-long walk up to the village of San Michele from Gardone. The path (waymarked from Vittoriale) misses out all the twists and turns of the road. The terrace at the hotel and restaurant *San Michele* – which serves good regional food – provides the perfect view *(closed Mon | 13 rooms | Via San Michele 26 | tel. 03 65 20 05 75 | Budget)*.

pulp for the production of paper. After about 30 mins you will reach the very well presented museum *Centro di Eccellenza di Maina Inferiore (May/June Sat/Sun 10am–5pm, July–Sept Tue–Fri 10.30am–4.30pm, Sat/Sun 10am–5pm, Oct Sat/Sun 2pm–4pm | www.valledellecartiere.it)*.

★ *Sant'Andrea Apostolo* church (1130–50) in Maderno is worth seeing even if you don't notice it at first as the more recent parish church opposite dominates the scene. The Romanesque chapel with its façade of pink, grey and white stripes is

Maritime still life: boats along the shore in Maderno

TOSCOLANO-MADERNO
(133 E2) (𝄞 G5)

The twin community (pop. 8000) lies slightly to the north, where the Toscolano feeds into the lake. Its upper course is the 'paper factory valley', which is well worth a visit. Back in the 14th century, the paper mills were already selling their wares throughout Europe, and later even in the Orient. A path passes by the ruins. It's best to start from the Gardesana by the turn to Gaino. Two millstones on the path can be seen. These were used to turn rags into

a jewel. The Lombardic/Romanesque detailing on the porch (fruit, leaf tendrils, plaited ornamentation) are testimony to the skill of the masons at that time. The harmonious interior is dominated by heavy pillars and columns with their imposing capitals.

The *Osteria del Boccondivino (closed lunchtimes and on Mon | Via Cavour 71 | tel. 03 65 64 25 12 | Moderate)* in Maderno specialises in fish. The ☺ *Ristorante San Marco (daily | Piazza San Marco | tel. 03 65 54 03 63 | www.hsmarco.it | Expensive)*, also located in Maderno, is an exclusive restaurant not far from the lake that has adopted the ideals of the 'slow-food' fraternity, producing regional dishes. Pizzas at lunchtime can be had at on the same square in *Cantinone (Piazza San Marco 49 | tel. 03 65 64 14 47 | Moderate)*. The tastefully renovated *Hotel Milano (Lungolago Zanardelli 12 | tel. 03 65 54 05 95 | www.hotelmilanomaderno.com | Moderate–Expensive)* is set far enough back from the through-road and has a beautiful view of the lake – and its own swimming pool. The *Hotel Vienna* in the Old Town does not have a view of the lake

GARGNANO

(133 F1) (ΩΩ G5) **Once you have had enough of all the tunnels on the west shore (if you come from the north) and can breathe out again having just passed through the last one, you will reach Gargnano (pop. 3000).**

The name actually applies to three little villages, each with a harbour, the first as lovely as the last. First of all you will come to the largest of the three, Gargnano itself, with its short lakeside promenade, followed by Villa and then Bogliaco, skirted

Cast a glance into the Baroque garden in the Villa Bettoni-Cazzago when driving past

(17 rooms | Via Garibaldi 43 | tel. 03 65 64 10 83 | www.gardavienna.it | Budget). Slightly less crowded than the Saturday market in Salò is the market on Thursdays in the main street in Toscolano. Information in Maderno: *Via Sacerdoti, corner Strada Statale | tel. 03 65 54 60 83 | www. provincia.brescia.it/turismo*

by the Gardesana road and each with just one one-way road leading into the village. Before the Gardesana was built in the 1930s, the most common way of getting about was by boat.

Today, there is literally nothing going on here – and that is why this stretch of the shore is so popular among regular visitors.

Hiking and strolling, swimming and dining – these are the reasons for coming here. And in the evening the same slow pace doesn't change. Gargnano got out of step once for a short time: during the Fascist period of the 'Republic of Salò', Mussolini lived here in the Villa Feltrinelli.

SIGHTSEEING

SAN FRANCESCO
The monastery and San Francesco's church in Gargnano were founded in 1289. The cloisters remains unaltered – a late Gothic, Romanesque treasure.

VILLA BETTONI-CAZZAGO
When the Gardesana Occidentale, the road down the west shore, was built, little consideration was given to cultural monuments. The road planners mercilessly chopped one of the most beautiful Baroque gardens on Lake Garda in two. As a result, however, today's holiday-maker has the possibility of taking a closer look at the park at the Villa Bettoni-Cazzago in Bogliaco. It is always open at the end of April, when a sale is held of selected plants *(www.ilgiardinodidelizia.it)*.

FOOD & DRINK

INSIDER TIP AL BACCARETTO
This little non-touristy *osteria* is located at the end of the promenade. Run by young proprietors, light snacks are accompanied by selected wines. *Closed Mon | Lungolago Zanardelli 10 | tel. 03 65 79 10 24 | Moderate*

MIRALAGO
Here you can sit under an awning, protected from the sun, and look out across the lake. The modest menu includes rocket salad with Parmesan or fine fish dishes. *Closed Tue | Lungolago Zanardelli 5 | tel. 03 65 71 12 09 | Budget–Moderate*

OSTERIA DEL RESTAURO
The pace of everyday life in Villa is gentle. If this is to your taste then the *osteria* is just right for you. The home-made tortellini, the spicy bacon *(lardo)* and the *antipasti* are all delicious. *Closed Wed | Piazza Villa 19 | tel. 0 36 57 26 43 | Moderate*

ALLO SCOGLIO
Here you can eat in a pretty garden in Bogliaco on the lakeside. The building is a former gatehouse to the Villa Bettoni-Cazzago. Fish is a speciality here. *Closed Fri | Via Barbacane 3 | tel. 0 36 57 10 30 | www.alloscoglio.it | Moderate*

SHOPPING

MARKET
A small market is held every second Wed on the harbourside in Gargnano.

LEISURE, SPORT & BEACHES

The ★ *Parco Fontanella*, to the north of the villages, is free of charge and has a beach. Here you can lie in the shade of the olive trees. For teenagers there is table tennis and techno music. Big carpark – also with no charge and the *OK-Surf* surfing school *(tel. 03 65 79 00 12 | www.oksurf.it)*.

ENTERTAINMENT

The pace in Gargnano is leisurely – which makes for regular visitors who prefer the quieter life. If you fancy an ice cream on the lakeside, the biggest and best are to be found in the *Bar Azzurra (Lungolago Zanardelli 9)*.

WHERE TO STAY

INSIDER TIP ANTICA CASCINA LIANO
The perfect retreat: in Liano, 600 m up, this fully renovated building with heavy

wooden ceilings and rustic interior is situated in farming country. This former farmhouse has extensive views of the lake. *6 flats | Via Liano 1 | tel. 0 36 57 28 70 | www. cascinaliano.it | Budget–Moderate*

GARDENIA AL LAGO
The building dates from the 1920s, the hotel from the '50s. The large rooms in this family-run hotel are simply furnished. The sun terrace, the garden and the breakfast room are particularly charming – and there is even a tiny private beach, too. *25 rooms | Via Colletta 53 | tel. 0 36 57 11 95 | www.hotel-gardenia.it | Moderate*

HOTEL DU LAC
This hotel, situated directly on the lake in Villa, is now in the third generation of the Arosio family. The antique furnishings in most rooms are lovely. *11 rooms | Via Colletta 21 | tel. 0 36 57 11 07 | www.hotel-dulac.it | Moderate*

LEFAY RESORT & SPA 😊
Magnificent 5-star complex high above the lake, ultra-modern, with floorboards of olive wood and a large pool, a huge spa facility extending over ¾ acres, and a top-class restaurant. When it was built, considerable thought was given to its ecological impact with the use of energy-saving technology. *90 rooms | Via A. Feltrinelli 118 | tel. 03 65 24 18 00 | www. lefayresorts.com | Expensive*

INSIDER **TIP** MEANDRO ☲
At first glance this modest-looking hotel may not appeal immediately, but the view will make up for that. All rooms (incl. the restaurant) in this family-run hotel have panoramic views of the lake. There is a swimming-pool with a roof and the large public beach is closeby. The ceramic artist Mariano Fuga *(www.marianofuga.it)* from Vicenza exhibits INSIDER **TIP** charming figurines in the building next door. *44 rooms | Via Repubblica 40 | tel. 0 36 57 11 28 | www.hotelmeandro.it | Moderate*

INFORMATION
Piazzale Boldini 2 | tel. 03 65 79 12 43 | www.gargnanosulgarda.it

OUTINGS
CAMPIONE (129 E5) *(ℳ H4)*
The old cotton mills in Campione in the parish of Tremosine, 10 km (6 mi) north of Gargnano, is being turned into a hotel resort with 200 flats and 10 villas. The

BOOKS & FILMS

▶ **Twilight In Italy** – in 1912 the English writer D. H. Lawrence hiked across the Alps to Italy and stayed in Gargnano with his lover. In this work he describes the days he spent on Lake Garda.

▶ **The International** – Tom Tykwer's thriller takes place in a number of places around the globe and in one scene a car disappears into a tunnel on a Mediterranean lake. Even if it's supposed to be somewhere else, it was filmed on Lake Garda.

▶ **Quantum of Solace** – The opening scene in this James Bond adventure was filmed on Lake Garda: a chase through the tunnels along the Gardesana.

structure of the workers' village is a listed monument and will be retained; the centre will be pedestrianised and there will be moorings for the flats, a hotel and spa facility. *Tel. 03 65 91 60 04 | www.campionedelgarda.it*

of the countryside. The lake has a wild beauty – not as blue and Mediterranean as Lake Garda but narrow and green.
It is worth taking a brief detour to the mountain village of *Magasa* at the end of the lake or turn off straight away to-

Swimming in Lake Idro is just as much fun

LAGO D'IDRO AND
INSIDER TIP ▶ LAGO DI VALVESTINO
(128 B–C 5–6) (*ḍ F–G 3–4*)
Lake d'Idro is to the west of Lake Garda in the mountains. The route begins in the centre of Gargnano, climbing steeply through hairpin bends. You soon leave behind the olive trees and enter an increasingly wooded area. The road leads steadily upwards until finally you find yourself heading towards a large dam of the *Lago di Valvestino*: the Toscolano stream is dammed behind this, making it possible to power the paper mills in the Toscolano-Maderno valley. There is a turnoff not far from the dam; you should take this in order to really enjoy a view

wards Capovalle. Follow the main road through the village and then down a steep hill though several hairpin bends. You will soon see the glittering lake – Lago d'Idro. The whole region has a certain mountainous Tyrolean feel but the villages are Italian with their narrow streets and Romanesque churches. In *Pieve Vecchia*, at the south end of the lake, you can stop for a break in one of the street cafés and watch the motorbikes pass or head for the *Pizzeria Milano (closed Tue Di | Via Trento 35 | tel. 03 65 82 33 91 | www.hotel-milano.bs.it, Budget)* for a bite to eat, which has a modest hotel attached. Information: *Via Trento 27 | Idro | tel. 0 36 58 32 24 | www.lagodidro.it*

The clinging terraces in Pieve: for those with a head for heights

MADONNA DI MONTECASTELLO ☆
(129 E6) (*Ⓜ H4*)

This hermitage, at an altitude of 700 m just a few miles to the north, is a popular place for day-trippers and pilgrims alike, with a wonderful view of Lake Garda and the mountains. *Daily mid March–Oct 9am–6pm | www.montecastello.org*

PIEVE (129 E5) (*Ⓜ H4*)

Tremosine and its main centre, Pieve, are just less than 20 km (12½ mi) north of Gargnano, high above the lake. Visitors are attracted by the ★ *terrazza del brivido* – and this is what the *Hotel Paradiso (22 rooms | tel. 03 65 95 30 12 | www.ter-razzadelbrivido.it | Moderate)* advertises with: its terrace really does jut frighteningly far over the lake below.

Near the terraces of hotel *Miralago (29 rooms | tel. 03 65 95 30 01 | www.mira lago.it | Budget)*, in which you can sleep directly above the sheer drop, there is a narrow path that takes you down the seemingly vertical cliff face to the lakeside below – and the bus. This path, the INSIDER TIP *Sentiero del Porto*, was once the only way down to the lake. Check with the tourist information office *(Piazza Marconi | tel. 03 65 95 31 85 | www.info tremosine.it)* before you set out to see if the path is open (sometimes its is closed due to falling rocks) and when buses run. For the very active, sample what is on offer at INSIDER TIP *Skyclimber (Thomas Engels | Via Dalco 3 | tel. 3 35 29 32 37 | www.skyclimber.it)*: this includes canyoning trips, mountain-bike training circuit and guided roped-climbing tours. There are also many possibilities for children.

SALÒ

MAP INSIDE BACK COVER
(133 D2) (*Ⓜ F6)* **Salò (pop. 11,000) has had the longest ★ promenade on Lake Garda for more than 100 years – it was built after an earthquake in 1901.**

In 2004 there was another earthquake which badly damaged a number of buildings. However, the lakeside promenade has since been widened and extended. It now runs for almost 3 km right round to the cemetery on the other side of the bay with its eye-catching cypresses. It is virtually car-free, with one café after another, and benches lining the shore. The little fishing boats bobbing about in the water are taken out into the lake in the mornings in search of what the gourmet restaurants in Salò later serve their guests: *lavarello* and *corregone* – Lake Garda whitefish. The town nestles in a bay at the southern end of the west shore and, even if today it is a busy little place, the former spa town still exudes a certain elegance.

Salò has always been wealthier than the neighbouring fishing villages. In 1377 is was declared the administrative centre for the west shore by the ruling Visconti of Milan. And in 1426 the Venetians named Salò the 'Magnifica Patria della Riviera'. Towards the end of the more recent period under Fascist rule, Mussolini raised Salò to the capital of the Fascist Socialist Republic.

dictator Benito Mussolini himself, as he was not only Head of State but also Foreign Minister and Chairman of the Council of Ministers at the same time. *Viale Landi 9 | www.laurinsalo.com*

ISOLA DEL GARDA

The island can be reached from Garda or from Salò: *April–Oct Tue and Thu 9.30am | 24 euros, incl. food and guided tour | departures from the port of Barbarano | reservation essential: tel. 32 83 84 92 26 | www.isoladelgarda.com*

SIGHTSEEING

HOTEL LAURIN

The Laurin is the most beautiful Art Deco building on the Lake. It is now an elegant hotel. If you only want a drink you can go into the lobby and marvel at the exquisite interior at your leisure. During the Fascist dictatorship, the building housed the Foreign Ministry for a time as well as the

PALAZZO DEL PODESTÀ

In the 16th century the old Town Hall from the 14th century was given a Venetian façade with an arcade, and it suits the building very well. However nothing of the original remains – the earthquake in 1901 also destroyed the Palazzo del Podestà.

The traffic-free promenade in Salò is perfect for a stroll and a shop

SALÒ

SANTA MARIA ANNUNZIATA ●
Salò is the only place on Lake Garda with a cathedral. Work started on the late Gothic building in 1453. A white Renaissance portal was later added to the plain brick façade. *Daily 8am–noon and 3pm–7pm | Piazza Duomo | www.parrocchiadisalo.it*

A homage to 'slow food' and to wine: La Campagnola

FOOD & DRINK

LA CAMPAGNOLA ☺
Angelo Dal Bon's restaurant is one of the best in the area offering regional cuisine according to the 'slow-food' principle. The food leaves as little to be desired as the unbeatable extensive wine list (570 different wines at the last count!). Reservation essential! *Closed Tue lunchtime and all day Mon | Via Brunati 11 | tel. 0 36 52 21 53 | www.lacampagnoladisalo.it | Expensive*

INSIDER TIP ▶ LA CASA DEL DOLCE
This is where you'll find probably the creamiest chocolate ice cream anywhere on the lake and you can watch it being made in the small parlour. *Piazza Duomo 1*

LOLLIPOP
This *yoghurteria* has the fruitiest ice cream in town, as lots of yoghurt is used – as the name implies. Twice as refreshing in summer! *Via Rocchetta 6*

LA ROSA DEI VENTI
In this very new little restaurant on the lakeside promenade considerable attention is paid to little details; homemade bread is served with all dishes from the small but choice menu. *Closed Tue | Lungolago Zanardelli 27 | tel. 03 65 29 07 47 | Moderate*

ANTICA TRATTORIA ALLE ROSE
Gianni Briarava serves only the very best in his contemporary-style restaurant. The classic *cucina gardesana* has been blended with new recipes ranging from pasta with beans, grilled horse meat or more refined fish dishes. *Closed Wed | Via Gasparo da Salò 33 | tel. 0 36 54 32 20 | www.roseorologio.it | Moderate–Expensive*

PASTICCERIA VASSALLI ●
Tasty sandwiches are on offer here, numerous cakes and *bacetti di Salò* – 'kisses from Salò' – delicious nut praliné chocolates. *Closed Tue in winter | Via San Carlo 84–86 | www.pasticceria-vassalli.it*

SHOPPING

The Old Town in Salò is perfect for shopping as it has many more shops than in smaller villages. Most are in *Via San Carlo*, that runs parallel to and slightly set back from the shore, between the cathedral to Piazza Zanelli.

BELLI

How about an Italian coffee machine for back home? There are plenty to choose from here – as well as Alessi's line of products. *Via San Carlo 72*

MARKET ★

Every Sat morning, south of the Old Town. This is one of the biggest markets on the lake. What you can't find here, you won't find anywhere else!

INSIDER TIP MELCHIORETTI

This grocery shop looks like a chemist's – and that's exactly what it used to be. Built in 1805, it has remained virtually unchanged since 1870 – except that instead of soap bars you'll find pesto and pasta on the wooden shelves. *Piazza Zanelli 11*

UBIK

This bookshop stocks modern Italian literature and a few books in English. *Via M. Butturini 28 a*

LEISURE, SPORT & BEACHES

When the promenade was extended two small beaches were made opposite the bay, not far from the cemetery. They are easy to pick out thanks to the distinctive row of cypresses. Closeby is the *Valtenesi* – a hilly area around Manerba. This is where there are a number of other places to swim: in *Porto San Felice* is a flat pebbly beach; the *Spiaggia della Rocca* is a large, free pebbly beach near the Rocca di Manerba; at *Pieve Vecchia* in Manerba there is a large stony beach with little shade but from here you can wade through the shallow water to the isle of San Biagio, popular with the younger generation. Pebbly and rocky beaches that are free of charge can be found in *Moniga*.

● One of the most beautiful places to jog on Lake Garda is the route around the local bay – the promenade is traffic-free. The best time is in the morning when relatively few people are out and about. Start wherever you like and head for the cypresses near the cemetery, then back to the cathedral and the far end of the pedestrian precinct. The round route is about 5 km (3.1 mi) long.

LOW BUDGET

▶ In many wine cellars along the *Strada dei Vini*, a glass of wine can be enjoyed at a cheaper price in summer if you're there before 8.30pm. Wine-tasting with a bite to eat for 5 euros. *www.stradadeivini.it*

▶ 200 shops offering reductions of up to 70 % on Bata, Nike, Versace & Co. can be found in Rodengo Saiano in the *Franciacorta Outlet Village (Tue–Sun 10am–8pm, Mon 2.30pm–8pm, in summer Sat/Sun until 9pm | 6 km beyond Brescia, motorway exit: Ospitaletto | www.franciacortaoutlet.it)*.

▶ Ask for a *Sport Card* at your hotel. With this you can get a discount when hiring sports equipment, for group-leaders and those accompanying them and for golf instructors, for mountain bikers, surfers, sailors, climbers and Nordic walking fans.

SALÒ

ENTERTAINMENT

The whole length of the Lungolago in Salò is given over to strolling in the evening. Just drift along, back and forth.

ABSOLUTE

This is really only for genuine night-owls as there is nothing going on before midnight. *On the lakeside in the bay opposite the promenade. Via Tavine 42*

AL BARETTO

An inconspicuous bar on the lakeside promenade – but the proprietor, Gigi, has the best selection of open wines, such as Bellavista, a sparkling wine from Franciacorta. This is where local wine-lovers meet for an aperitif or for a midnight drink. *Lungolago Zanardelli 46*

ESTATE MUSICALE GASPARO DA SALÒ

Classical music concerts are held on the square in front of the cathedral on summer evenings (July/August).

WHERE TO STAY

AGRITURISMO IL BAGNOLO

Fancy a holiday on a farm just a few miles from Lake Garda? Located way above the lake and for those who love the peace and quiet, it's ideal. Milk is fresh from the cow, cold meat and cheese are all produced on the farm. *9 rooms | Bagnolo di Serniga | tel. 0 36 52 02 90 | www.ilbagnolo.it | Moderate*

BELLERIVE

After the marina was expanded, this hotel was built. It has a pretty location on the promenade, a lovely garden and an even more beautiful view from the little balconies. *49 rooms | Via Pietro da Salò 11 | tel. 03 65 52 04 10 | www.hotelbellerive.it | Expensive*

BED & BREAKFAST AI COLLI

This new building with a wonderful view of the lake is situated in a quiet residential area above the through-road. *5 rooms | Via Carla Motari 6 | tel. 0 36 52 00 11 | www.bblagodigarda.it | Budget*

HOTEL DUOMO

This very friendly hotel is next to the cathedral on the long lakeside promenade. *22 rooms | Lungolago Zanardelli 63 | tel. 0 36 52 10 26 | www.hotelduomosalo.it | Expensive*

HOTEL GAMBERO

This was one of the cheapest hotels in Salò for some time, then it became almost derelict. It has now been beautifully renovated and re-opened. Reserve one of the quieter rooms with a view of the lake. *25 rooms | Piazza Carmine 1 | tel. 03 65 29 09 41 | www.gamberohotel.it | Moderate*

INFORMATION

Piazza Sant'Antonio 4 | tel. 0 36 52 14 23 | www.rivieradeilimoni.it

OUTINGS

MANERBA DEL GARDA
(133 D3) (*𝄞 F6*)

A INSIDER**TIP** lovely easy walk to the ⚜ *Rocca di Manerba* starts from this little town (population 5000) some 10 km (6 mi) south of Salò. Either start at the carpark below the centre of Montinelle and follow the Via del Melograno or drive up this same narrow road as far as the carpark next to the nature reserve. From here is it just a short walk to the ruins. Work on excavating this site has recently been taken up again and the low remains of the old castle walls have been well renovated. A wonderful panorama can be enjoyed from here.

Salò in the evening: life at a slower pace on the west shore

En route to the Rocca there is a new *agriturismo* farmhouse holiday address: *La Filanda (26 flats | Via del Melograno 35 | tel. 03 65 55 10 12 | www.agriturismo-lafilanda.it | Moderate)*. If you like things to be more peaceful, try *Agriturismo Masserino (Via Masserino 2 | Puegnago | tel. 03 65 65 17 57 | www.masserino.it | Moderate)* which lies halfway between Manerba and San Felice. There is no restaurant here but oil and wine can be bought directly from the farmer. The large hotel *La Quiete (35 rooms | Via del Rio 92 | tel. 03 65 55 11 56 | www.laquietepark hotel.it | Moderate)* is an elegant place to stay. It is also worth exploring the area around Manerba if you want to buy olive oil as many of the producers have their own farm shops.

SAN FELICE DEL BENACO
(133 D3) (*ⓜ F6*)

Most campsites on Lake Garda are to be found between Salò and Desenzano; hotels are noticeably fewer in number here. The beaches tend to be pretty full and, although access to most of the beaches not owned by the campsites is free of charge, the carparks are not. On top of that, many day-visitors come here at the weekends. But away from the lake you can wind your way between vineyards and olive groves.

The centre of San Felice (pop. 3400) and its churches are worth a detour. There is a small beach near Porto Portese for swimming.

Homemade pasta and a massive serving of fish starters are available at the *Ristorante Osvaldo (closed Tue | Piazzale Marinai d'Italia 5 | tel. 0 36 56 21 08 | Moderate)*. The *Park Hotel Casimiro Village* is a huge hotel with a matching swimming pool (*198 rooms | Via Porto Portese 22 | tel. 03 65 62 62 62 | www. bluhotels.it | Moderate)*. Good olive oil can be found at *La Verità (Via delle Gere 2)*.

TRIPS & TOURS

The tours are marked in green in the road atlas, pull-out map and on the back cover

1

BY CABLE-CAR TO THE TOP AND THEN ON FOOT

● This 'green' tour, starting in Malcesine, doesn't completely do without means of transport – but a difference in altitude of 1700 m doesn't necessarily have to be done on foot: that really would be a bit too strenuous. So let's take the cable-car and ride to the top of Monte Baldo. Once there, you can hike to your heart's content.

The journey from the cable-car station in Malcesine → p. 36 is stunning in its own right. You have a wonderful view of the lake from the rotating cabin and there's no scrambling for the best places next to the window *(cable-car, daily 8am until 5/6/7pm, depending on the season | return journey 18, one-way 12 euros | tel. 04 57 40 02 06 | www.funiviedelbaldo.it)*. Once at the top, you'll have to gasp first – the panoramic views are simply breath-taking (assuming you have chosen a day when the weather is good!). The Brenta Group, endless mountain ranges and, far below, the lake. If you can't take it all in at once, just find a place on the terrrace at the cable-car station and enjoy the panorama – perhaps with a cappuccino.

The walk you chose rather depends on how fit you are. The most challenging route is the one to Cima Valdritta. This takes

Photo: Lago di Toblino

There's a lot to discover in the mountains above Lake Garda and on a short trip to Trento

you along the ridge of Monte Baldo towards the south. Beyond the cable-car station it drops down slightly to start with into the dip called the **Bocca di Tratto Spino**. You cannot miss the path; it's well sign-posted with a red-white-red marker and the number 651.

There is another walk to **Cima delle Pozzette** (2128 m, 6982 ft), but this shouldn't be attempted in light shoes or flip-flops. The path beyond the Cima delle

Pozzette becomes increasingly more demanding and includes several simple climbing stretches. If you're not up to this, don't try and carry on to **Cima Valdritta** (2218 m; 7277 ft). The path to Cima Valdritta and to the Rifugio Telegrafo hut were originally made by the army. Parts of the route were blasted out of the rock face during World War I. The two man-made caves below the summit of Valdritta date from this period. When out walking, take a close look at the flora. The area around the summit of Monte Baldo peaked out above the sea of glaciers during the Ice Age and, as a result, plants have survived that are not found anywhere else, such as the *anemone Baldense*.

It's best to return to the cable-car station at the summit by the same route. There is a steeper path behind Cima Valdritta down to Doss Castion and from there on towards the half-way station or down to Malcesine (Cima Valdritta–Malcesine: approx 5 hours). You should plan one whole day for this tour.

If you don't want to hike all day long, you can choose between several shorter circular routes. The easiest is towards the north, and leads slightly uphill from the cable-car station as far as the mountain hut **La Capannina** where you can have something to eat and drink. It then continues in a northerly direction along the ridge. After approx. 30 mins you will reach the **Cime di Ventrar** ☀ viewpoint and can look down over Riva.

In summer, you can also plump for the 'Sentiero delle Malghe sul Monte Baldo con Gusto' – a walk with several stops for food. For 23 euros you can buy a voucher and hike from Baita dei Forti to four summer farms and restaurants along the route. Vouchers can be bought at Baita dei Forti at the cable-car station at the top of the mountain.

Another waymarked walk is from the station at the summit down to the **half-way station San Michele**, along a route with lots of hairpins. You can either stop for a while or stay the night at the **Locanda Monte Baldo** (*daily | 11 rooms | tel. 04 57 40 16 79 | www.locandamontebaldo.com | Budget–Moderate*), which has a swimming pool and a terrace where you can stretch out those tired legs under the table.

If you can't get enough of the view from the top of Monte Baldo, you can stay the

Testimony to an elegant past: the bell-tower and castle in Arco

night there too. This is something quite special as, in the evening, you'll have the otherwise heavily visited Monte Baldo all to yourself. The summit restaurant Baita dei Forti → p. 41 is run by Marco Menotti and his brother. There are 6 rooms for overnight guests. The view from this altitude of the lake at night with the flickering lights along the shore is quite a sight.

2 ALONG THE SARCA VALLEY TO TRENTO

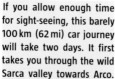

If you allow enough time for sight-seeing, this barely 100 km (62 mi) car journey will take two days. It first takes you through the wild Sarca valley towards Arco. You then pass two lakes before finally reaching Trento – a city with a magnificent past and the capital of Trentino. On the following day you return to Lake Garda by way of Rovereto with its famous museum for contemporary art. It is also possible to use public transport for the journey. In any case, the inner-city of Rovereto is closed to traffic and parking spaces are hard to find and expensive. If you are mainly interested in Trento, you can take the bus to Rovereto and change to the train there or travel all the way from Riva to Trento by bus (a stopover in Arco is possible).

The tour begins between Torbole and Riva del Garda directly beneath Monte Brione. After a few miles, you reach Arco. You can still see that the town (pop. 16,500) has an interesting past; the villas and hotels of the once up-market spa were built around the old mountain village.

It is best to park your car and walk up to the 🔍 castle (daily April–Sept 10am–7pm, Oct–March 10am–4pm), from where you have the best view. The climb begins opposite the church and a sign points the way to the castello. The castle can be seen from afar dominating the town. In 1495, Albrecht Dürer painted it during his journey through Italy and a postcard of this scene can be bought in most of the village's shops. In 1703, the French duke General Vendôme slighted the castle. Arco's church seems much too big, almost overwhelming the village. It was built in the Palladian style between 1613 and 1671 and is one of the most famous late Renaissance buildings in Trentino.

Leaving the Old Town, you come to the INSIDER TIP Parco Arciducale (daily 8am–7pm, Oct–March 9am–4pm | www.comune. arco.tn.it/vivere/Parchi/Arboreto/Arboreto. aspx): the Habsburg archdukes had the garden planted with trees and shrubs at the turn to the 20th century. The Tourist Information Office (Viale delle Palme 1 | tel. 04 64 53 22 55 | www.gardatrentino. it) is located near the former spa building. If you feel peckish, the Cantina Marchetti (closed Mon | Piazza Marchetti | tel. 04 64 51 62 33 | Budget) serves enormous pizzas in the courtyard of an old palazzo. Not only mountain-bikers enjoy the bicicletta – a mixture of Campari and Prosecco – served in the INSIDER TIP Caffè Conti d'Arco (closed Thu | Piazza Marchetti 3).

The journey continues on route 45 to Dro. Be sure not to miss the turn-off to Lago di Cavedine. After a few bends further up the hill, you will reach Marocche – an unchanged wild landscape. In primeval times, a massive rock fall crashed down into the valley and the huge boulders lie scattered around like building blocks for giant children. Follow the twisty road and on a hairpin bend to the right, turn left to Lago di Cavedine. There is a narrow road along the lake, a few picnic places and a lot of people fishing.

You reach the main road to Trento in Pietramura and drive past another lovely lake: Lago di Toblino. You can walk across a dyke to the castle with its striking towers on an island in the lake. Its core was part of a 12th-century fortress and it was transformed into a comfortable residence by Prince-Bishop Madruzzo in the 16th century. Today, there is a good restaurant there: INSIDER TIP ▶ *Ristorante Castel Toblino (closed Tue and Nov–Feb | Via Caffaro 1 | tel. 04 61 86 40 36 | www.casteltoblino. com | Moderate–Expensive)*.

After another (20 km; 12½mi) you reach Trento (pop. 115,000). The Council of Trent, which was convened to save the Catholic Church from Luther's reformation, made the city on the river Adige famous. Bernardo Clesio, Prince-Bishop of Trento and a cunning politician with local interests at heart, made an effort in the 15th century to make Trento the venue of the Council. He had the medieval fortified town transformed into a Renaissance city and the council took place in Trento between 1545 and 1563.

You should start your tour of the city in the massive Castello Buonconsiglio *(May–Nov Tue–Sun 10am–6pm, Dec–April 9.30am–5pm | www.buonconsiglio.it)*, on which Clesio left his mark: his coat-of-arms – two lions on a red-and-white background – can be seen everywhere in the castle that forms part of the town's defensive wall. As the seat of government of the prince-bishops of Trento, the castle consists of three sections: Castelvecchio, Magno Palazzo and Giunta Albertiana. Passing through the rooms, one becomes intoxicated by the magnificent colours of the frescoes. On no account should you miss the Eagle Tower with its Gothic frescoes of the months. This cycle of pictures is unique in the history of art and was created between 1390 and 1407 by the Bohemian painter Wenceslaus.

Follow the Via San Marco into the Old Town. The Palazzo del Monte, a 16th-century Renaissance building is located on the corner of the Via del Suffragio. The Palazzo Galasso is another grand townhouse which Georg Fugger from Augsburg had erected in 1602. The San Francesco Saverio church, dating from the first half of the 18th century, stands on the corner of the Via Roma and Via Belenzani. It is considered the most important Baroque building in Trento. The Via Belenzani leads to the Piazza Duomo. On the left, the renovated Palazzo Geremia from the 15th century is particularly striking with its Venetian frescoes. This is opposite the Palazzo Thun, which has been the seat of the city administration since 1873.

Piazza Duomo, with its Neptune Fountain from 1768 in the centre, is one of the most beautiful squares in Italy. The cathedral itself, a massive Gothic house of worship, was constructed around 1100 on the foundations of an older church and the grave of Saint Vigilio. The foundations of the 6th-century basilica have been excavated under the choir in the interior of the cathedral. The low arcades of the Case Rella, opposite the cathedral, bear witness to the alpine heritage of the town.

You have the best view of the heart of the city from the Caffè Italia *(Piazza Duomo 7)*. It is unlikely that any inn is much older than the Ristorante al Vò *(closed Sun | Vicolo del Vò 11 | tel. 04 61 98 53 74 | www. ristorantealvo.it | Moderate)*. The first *osteria* in Trento was opened here in 1345 and traditional Trentino cooking can still be had here today. The brochure 'Osterie Tipiche Trentine' can be obtained from the tourist office and gives information on other traditional restaurants. All of the restaurants included – among them the Antica Trattoria Due Mori *(closed Mon | Via San Marco 11 | tel. 04 61 98 42 51 | www. ristoranteduemori.com | Moderate)* – only use produce from the Trentino region. You can stay in the centre of town – yet inexpensively – in the hotel Venezia *(40 rooms | Piazza Duomo 45 | tel. 04 61*

23 4114 | www.hotelveneziatn.it | Budget).
Ask for a room with a view of the cathedral. Information: Via Manci 2 | tel. 04 61
21 60 00 | www.apt.trento.it

You pass **Rovereto** on your way back along strada statale 12. It is worth stopping in this town (pop. 37,500) in the Adige valley most important representatives of this art movement, moved to Rovereto in 1919. His house was turned into a museum but there was not enough room there for his complete bequest – which provided the impetus for the new museum building. The museum's historical holdings com-

Spectacular architecture for contemporary art: MART in Rovereto

to visit the **military museum** (Museo Storico Italiano della Guerra | Tue–Fri 10 am–6 pm, Sat/Sun 9.30am–6.30pm | Via Castelbarco 7 | www.museodellaguerra. it) and the ultramodern Museum for Modern and Contemporary Art, the ★ **Museo di Arte Moderna e Contemporanea di Trento e Rovereto MART** (Tue–Thu and Sat/Sun 10am–6pm, Fri 10am–10pm | Corso Bettini 43 | english.mart.trento.it). The focus here is on 20th and 21st-century modern Italian art. With more than 15,000 works, the displays at MART are changed at regular intervals. It includes the most important collection of futuristic art in Italy and a research centre on Futurism. Fortunato Depero, one of the prise more than 80,000 documents such as correspondence, manuscripts, drawings, photographs and newspaper cuttings. On top of these, there are also 60,000 books, catalogue and magazines, that represent a good cross-section of 20th-century art and culture. The new building was designed by the architect Mario Botta from Tecino, who was faced with having to solve the problem of integrating a large new building in a compact Old Town. He placed the museum's rooms, spread out over three storeys, around a massive, round agora, with a glass dome on top. This central area is used for events for up to 1200 people. From Rovereto, it is a 30 min journey back to the lake again.

SPORTS & ACTIVITIES

Lake Garda is a sportsman's paradise: test your stamina wind and kite-surfing, mountain biking, hiking and climbing in, on or above the lake.

ADVENTURE SPORTS

It is not possible to indulge in adventure sports without professional instruction. Canyoning is one of them. Here, the venturesome hurl themselves down waterfalls in their neoprene suits and crash helmets, held only by a rope, and pursue raging torrents downstream. The following establishments provide guided tours: *Wet Way (Viale Rovereto 44 | Riva del Garda | tel. 33 56 39 90 63 | www.wetway.net), Multisport (Via San Pietro Paolo 5 | Arco | tel. 04 64 50 44 90 | www.multisport3.com), Thomas Engels (Via Dalco 3 | Tremosine | tel. 03 65 91 70 41 | www.aktivcenter-lagodigarda. com), Canyon Adventures (Via Matteotti 122 | Torbole | tel. 04 64 50 54 06 | www. canyonadventures.it).*

CLIMBING & HIKING

No matter whether you prefer day trips in the mountains, rambling over the hills or strolling along the shore: if you like being on the move, you won't get bored on Lake Garda. The peak of ● Monte Baldo is, of course, one of the main goals for hikers. There are two mountaineering centres in

An adventure playground for adults:
water sports fans and mountain lovers can
really let off steam on Lake Garda

Arco; both organise climbing courses, hikes and canyoning tours: *Ufficio delle Guide Alpine (Via Santa Caterina 40 | tel. 04 64 50 70 75 | www.guidealpinearco.com)* and *Friends of Arco (Piazza 3 Novembre 6 | tel. 04 64 53 28 28 | www.friendsofarco.it).* The INSIDER TIP ► *Rock Master* climbing competition in mid-September, which attracts the global elite of free climbers, is also a real spectacle for on-lookers *www. rockmaster.com.*

CYCLING & MOUNTAIN BIKING

● The north is the most popular area for ambitious cyclists; the Riva tourist office can supply first-rate information. The ★ *Bike Festival* is held around Riva in late April/early May. The highlight of the event is the strenuous bike marathon. A similar competition is held in Limone in October *(www.bike-xtreme.com).*

Monte Baldo is the most popular destination among fit bikers. Those who want to avoid the grind of riding uphill take the cable-car from Malcesine, **INSIDER TIP** which also transports bikes at certain times. You can not only hire bikes from *Bike Xtreme* at the cable-car station in the valley *(Via Navene Vecchia 10 | tel. 04 57 40 01 05 | www.bikeapartments.com)*, they will even transport them to the top of Monte Baldo. Guided tours are available as well.

The province of Verona has introduced the *Bus & Bike* service for the summer months: you take the scheduled bus service, which also transports bikes, up to Novezza or Prada and from there it is downhill all the way.

It is an ambitious project creating a continous bike path from Riva to Sirmione. However, Monte Baldo and its foot-hills literally stand in the way. There is not much room between the mountain, the road and the lake. Nevertheless, the project is making progress. It is already possible to pedal in safety for many miles alongside the road to the north and south of Malcesine. Building is also underway in Bardolino and you can cycle beside the lake between Cisano and Lazise. Unfortunately, the narrow tunnels in the northern-most section still remain a problem.

DIVING

Diving fans do not get treated too badly on Lake Garda either. Instead of coral reefs, they dive for sunken galleons and a glowing statue of the Madonna takes the place of brightly-coloured fish. The 13m-high illuminated figure was anchored at a depth of 18 m (60 ft) on the lake bottom on the initiative of the Brenzone diving club.

Diving centres offering courses and tours can be found in Riva, Salò, Torri del Benaco and Desenzano. *Athos Diving (Assenza di Brenzone | Via Gardesana 54 | Tel. 04 56 59 00 15 | www.athos-diving.com)* organises courses.

GOLF

The 27-hole golf course *Ca' degli Ulivi (tel. 04 56 27 90 30 | www.golfcadegliulivi.it)* is located in *Marciaga* near Costermano, not far from Garda. There is an 18-hole course near Gargnano: *Golf Club Bogliaco (Via del Golf 21 | tel. 03 65 64 30 06 | www.golfbogliaco.com)*. The 5-star gold resort *Palazzo Arzaga Hotel Golf & Saturnia Spa (84 rooms | Carzago di Calvagese della Riviera | tel. 0 30 68 06 00 | www.palazzo arzaga.it | Expensive)* is 15 km (9¼mi) south-west of Salò. Near Peschiera you'll find the beautifully situated *Parc Hotel Paradiso & Golf Resort (Via Coppo 2 b | Castelnuovo | tel. 04 56 40 58 11 | www.golfclubparadiso.it)*. Detailed information on golf courses can be found under www.*garda-golf.com*.

MARATHON

Running competitions are becoming increasingly popular on the lake. A marathon from Limone to Malcesine is now held at the end of September *(tel. 03 65 91 37 11 | www.lakegardamarathon.com)*. The Garda Trentino Half Marathon takes place on the second weekend in November in the Sarca valley. The route runs from Riva to Arco via Torbole and back.

RIDING

Riding and horseback tours are organised by *Agriturismo il Bosco (Puegnago sul Garda | tel. 0 36 55 55 05), Scuderia Castello (Toscolano-Maderno | tel. 03 65 64 41 01 | www.scuderiacastello.it), Club Ippico San Giorgio Arco (tel. 34 84 43 83 07 | www.clubippicosangiorgio.it), Ranch La Betulla (Vesio di Tremosine | tel. 03 65 91 72 56)*.

More information on the internet, e.g. under *www.lagodigardamagazine.com/horse-riding-centres-garda-lake.aspx*

SAILING

Even though windsurfing made Lake Garda famous among young sport fans, sailing has a much longer history here. The *Centomiglia (www.centomiglia.it)* – a 100-mile-long regatta – which starts in Bogliaco on the second Saturday in September, is famous.

WIND- & KITESURFING

The supreme discipline on Lake Garda, which is particularly well suited for windsurfing because its northern section emerges from a narrow mountain valley through which regular – and sometimes quite strong – winds blow like from a jet. The Sover, also called the Pelér – a north wind – brings out the watersports fans early in the morning. Around midday Ora – a strong south wind – takes over. Apart from these two 'main' winds, there are a number of other regular winds too. Torbole on the north shore is unquestionably the surfers' Mecca; in Riva, the conditions are also suitable for beginners. One advantage: motorboats are not permitted in the Trentino section of the lake. In addition to Torbole, the surfing schools and centres renting boards are mainly concentrated in Riva, Malcesine and Gargnano. ● Kitesurfing is quickly gaining in popularity. The acrobatic jumps also appeal to those watching. Most surf schools have included this trendy sport in there portfolio.

Without doubt: windsurfing is the no. 1 sport on Lake Garda

TRAVEL WITH KIDS

Lake Garda is a particularly child-friendly holiday area in especially child-friendly Italy. In the south, the lake is so shallow that parents can calmly let their offspring splash around.

On the other hand, the north shore is more interesting for older children; they can watch the wind-surfers before taking a lesson to see if they like it or not – this is possible in most wind-surfing schools if you call beforehand.

The following four beaches in the south-east corner of the lake are particularly suitable for children: *Punta Cornicello* (small, but with trees and a playground) in Bardolino, *the beach near the port in Pacengo* (flat, coarse sand beach, a few

trees, paddle-boat hire, showers and a bar), *Lido di Ronchi* (flat sandy beach with grassy areas and trees, a bar and showers) not far from Gardaland in Castelnuovo del Garda, as well as the *Spiaggia Comunale* in *Santa Maria di Lugana* near the Sirmione peninsula (wide stretch of grassy shore-line, playground, paddle boat and sun-shade hire).

The large *Spiaggia Sabbiono* (lots of trees, pebbly beach, artificial bathing islands) on the north shore in the centre of Riva is better suited to older children because the water quickly becomes deep. One beach that is also popular with young Italians is *Spiaggia Parco Fontanella* near Gargnano, built like an open-air swimming

Safari, aquatic and amusement parks provide a change. But don't forget the range of things the lake naturally has to offer!

pool, with showers, bars, table tennis and table soccer. In addition, there are many playgrounds in Riva.

NORTH SHORE

CLIMBING COURSES FOR CHILDREN
(130 C3) *(⋒ I–K2)*
The *Friends of Arco* climbing school *(Arco–Prabi | tel. 04 64 53 28 28 | www.friendso-farco.it)* offers various courses.

INSIDER TIP ▶ MUSEO DEL CENTRO VISITATORI PARCO ALTO GARDA BRESCIANO (129 E5) *(⋒ H4)*
The perfect programme for a rainy day: the geology, flora, fauna and life in the region are explained this brand-new well-laid out museum. Ask for the English translations at the reception desk. *March–mid Dec Sat–Thu 10am–5pm | 5 euros, 7 for a guided tour, children under 14 years 4 euros | Tignale | Prabione*

MUSEO DELLE PALAFITTE
(129 E3) *(ɱ H2)*

The children will also find the lake dwelling museum in Molina di Ledro on Lake Ledro above Riva exciting. They can even see the remains of food that was excavated from the peaty mud near the shore in the vividly decorated museum. There is a replica of a pile dwelling on the lake – there you can well imagine how the predecessors of the Italians lived. *March–June and Sept–Nov Tue–Sun 9am–5pm, July, Aug daily 10am–6pm | 3 euros, children 2 euros | www.palafitteledro.it*

WIND-SURFING COURSE FOR KIDS
(130 C3–4) *(ɱ I2)*

When youngsters attempt to begin wind-surfing with their parents' boards, they usually find the rigs too heavy. The Vasco Renna surfing school in Torbole offers courses with equipment specially designed for children. *Tel. 04 64 50 59 93 | www.vascorenna.com*

EAST SHORE

BENACUS FREE TIME
(135 D4) *(ɱ I7)*

A leisure park in Pastrengo with a go-cart track, skittles, billiards, a pizzeria and a so-called 'Kids' Paradise' with bouncy castle, slides, things to ride on and other similar attractions. Entrance free: you pay for the individual attractions separately. *Wed–Sun 2pm–midnight | Via Gardesana 11 | www.benacus.it*

CANEVA-WORLD
(134 C4) *(f H7)*

In the leisure park at the southern end of Lazise with its water park, Movieland, Rock Café and 'Mister Movie Studios', there is also a restaurant with medieval shows. *Mid April–June and early–mid Sept, closed on varying days 10am–6pm, July/Aug daily 10am–7pm | 24 euros, children under 1.40 m (4 ft 8 in) 19 euros, up to 1 m (3 ft 3 in) free | Via Fossalta 58 | www.canevaworld.it*

Gardaland on the east shore: a magnet for the young and young at heart between 2 and 70!

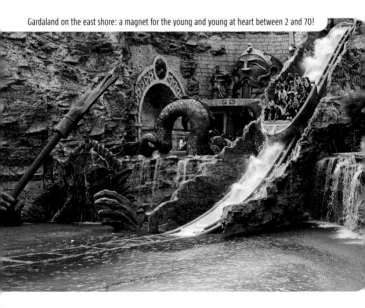

GARDALAND (134 C5) (*⋔ H8*)

The most famous and oldest amusement park (founded in 1975) on Lake Garda. The park offers entertainment à la Disneyland and this makes it a destination that not only appeals to the youngsters but also offers many attractions for older children and grown-ups: the adventurous take the Magic Mountain roller coaster with its two loopings, the fountains and laser effects at the water show are astounding, and the little ones can take a ride in a 'coffee cup' through the dwarf world. The park is often hopelessly overcrowded at weekends and your patience will be tested on the approach roads. Opening times vary considerably. Please check beforehand. *Daily April–Sept, generally 10am–6pm, Oct–Jan sometimes 10am–6pm, daily mid June–mid Sept 10qm–11pm or 9am–midnight | 36 euros, children (2–10 years) 29 euros | www.gardaland.it*

INSIDER TIP ▶ JUNGLE ADVENTURE PARK

(134 C2) (*⋔ H5*)

Clamber around the tree canopy on wooden boardwalks in this aerial ropeway and adventure park above San Zeno di Montagna. *May–mid Sept daily 10am–7pm, April and mid Sept–Oct Sat/Sun 10am–6pm | depending on the route chosen 12–28 euros | www.jungleadventure.it*

PARCO NATURA VIVA

(135 D5) (*⋔ I7*)

You can watch rhinoceroses, lions and tigers in the wild, from the safety of your car, in this safari park, located between Pastrengo and Bussolengo in the area beyond Lazise. You must however keep the windows closed! In the neighbouring zoo the children will particularly like the dinosaur park – even though the primeval beasts are only replicas. A new-comer among the 250 other species of animal is a sloth that that can now enjoy its free-dom. Up until now it had been kept in a cage. The previous owner tried to sell the animal online: the park heard about it and is now looking after it. *Daily March–Nov, opening times vary, but generally from around 9am–6pm | combined tickets for Safari Park and Zoo 17.50 euros, children under 12, 14 euros, June–Sept 19/16 euros | www.parconaturaviva.it*

RIOVALLI

(135 D4) (*⋔ H7*)

Those who are not satisfied with just bathing and hanging around can travel to the Riovalli aquatic park on the outskirts of Bardolino. *June–Aug Mon–Fri 9.30am–7pm, Sat/Sun 9am–7pm | 8 euros (Sun 10 euros), children 6 euros (Sun 7 euros) | Cavaion Veronese | in Fosse on the main road near Affi | www.riovalli.it*

SEA LIFE GARDALAND

(134 C5) (*⋔ H8*)

The large aquarium on the same site as the leisure park shows what's going on in the world's oceans but also in Lake Garda. The 35 main basins are alive with crabs and starfish, sharks and rays. Sealions can also be seen in one of the outdoor basins as can a coral reef. *Daily in summer 10am–6pm, in winter Mon–Fri 10am–4pm, Sat/Sun 10am–6pm | 15 euros, children 9.50 euros | www.gardaland.it*

SOUTH SHORE

FATTORIA DIDATTICA PARCO GIARDINO SIGURTÀ (O) (*⋔ O*)

This historic farm in the park has been adapted into a teaching farm with native breeds of chicken, duck and turkey, and donkeys and sheep from the Lessini mountains in the area. *Daily April–Sept 9am–6pm, March and Oct 9am–5pm| 12 euros, children (5–14 years) 6 euros | Valeggio sul Mincio | www.sigurta.it/fattoria.asp*

FESTIVALS & EVENTS

Especially in the high season there are any number of festivals and celebrations going on. Keep an eye out for posters or just ask at the tourist information office.

HOLIDAYS

1 Jan *Capodanno*, **6 Jan** *Epifania*, **Easter Sunday** and **Easter Monday** *(Pasqua and Pasquetta)*, **25 April** Liberation Day *(Liberazione)*, **1 May** *Festa del Lavoro*, **2 June** National Holiday *(Festa della Repubblica)*, **15 Aug** *Ferragosto*, **1 Nov** *Ognissanti*, **8 Dec** *Immacolata Concezione*, **25 Dec** *Natale*, **26 Dec** *Santo Stefano*

FESTIVALS & EVENTS

EASTER
A ▶ *candle-lit procession* depicting the Passion of Christ takes place at night on Venerdì Santo (Good Friday) in the Old Town in Limone and the Stations of the Cross are visited in the form of a ▶ *Passion play* in Castelletto di Brenzone.

LATE APRIL/EARLY MAY
▶ *Bike festival* in Riva – see section 'Sports & Activities'.

MAY
Little Red Riding Hood procession for families: ▶ *Cappuccetto Rosso* held on 1 May in Costermano. Boys are given a wolf's costume, girls are disguised as Little Red Riding Hood and then it's off on a trip into the land of fairy tales. *www.mangiafiaba.it*
The ▶ *Festa del Vino Chiaretto* takes place in Bardolino with a street party.
The residents of Torri honour their patron saint ▶ *San Filippo Neri* with a night-time sailing regatta on 26 May.

JUNE
White wine is served free of charge in Limone on the Piazza Garibaldi one weekend in June during the ▶ *Festa Popolare del Lago*. Fish from the lake can be had too. The beginning of summer is celebrated at the ▶ *Festa della Musica* in Arco on 21 June. The Old Town is brought to life by open-air events by hobby artists and professional musicians.

JULY/AUGUST
In the theater Vittoriale degli Italiani in Gardone, there are ▶ ● *concerts and open-air performances*. ▶ *Concerts* and plays take place in Malcesine on an open-air

Culture, sport and religion – the festivals and regattas for cyclists and sailors are enjoyed to the full

stage next to the castle ▶ *(Malcesine e l'Europa)*, while in the arena in Verona, the ▶ *opera festival* is held.

The INSIDER TIP ▶ *Serata Suoni e Sapori Antichi* takes place one Sunday in July in Limone. You can sample local specialities and wines at various stands for just 15 euros accompanied by music. The ▶ *Suoni e Sapori Antichi nell'Uliveto* in August is similar.

On 26 July in Malcesine there is a ▶ *torch-light procession* in honour of Saints Benignus and Carus.

▶● INSIDER TIP ▶ *Musica Riva*, an international series of concerts by young musicians, is held in the second half of July in the castle. www.musicarivafestival.com Street festivals mark the ▶ *Carnevale del Sole* on the last Sat in July in Salò.

Riva holds a large festival in August with processions and open-air performances, crowned by the ▶ *Notte di Fiaba*, a firework display on the lake. www.nottedifiaba.it

SEPTEMBER

The regatta ▶ *Centomiglia* in Bogliaco takes place on the second weekend in September. www.centomiglia.it

In mid September Torri del Benaco celebrates the ▶ *Carnevale Settembrino* with processions and street artists.

In Riva, Arco and Torbole wine and local produce can be sampled during the ▶ *grape festival*.

OCTOBER

The ▶ *Ciottolando con Gusto* – a wine-tasting event in Malcesine with culinary highlights – takes place in early October. www.ciottolando.com

The ▶ *Bixe Xtrem* mountain-bike competition around Limone, Riva and Ledro is only for the very fit! www.bikex-treme.com Drink till you drop at the ▶ *Festa dell'Uva* in Bardolino. Large firework display in the evening.

LINKS, BLOGS, APPS & MORE

LINKS

▶ www.rivieradeilimoni.it is an excellent site with information about the places on the western shore from Limone to Desenzano. It has listings for hotels, restaurants, cultural events, religious festivals well as webcams from each of the villages and some online maps.

▶ www.gardatrentino.it a site run by a consortium of villages on the southern coast to promote the hospitality industry in their area. The site includes special offers, suggested routes, themed holidays, weather updates as well as the usual accommodation, events and restaurant listings.

▶ www.vistgarda.com is the official tourism website of Lake Garda. The listings include hotels, apartments, holiday farms and camp sites.

▶ www.gardapass.com is an online hotel booking site specialising in the east coast area. It also has other useful information about internal transport links, local museums and places of interest.

BLOGS & FORUMS

▶ www.lake-garda-revealed.com this is a good site for useful tips and up to the minute details on activities taking place around the lake. The site has lots of links to other web pages, topical news and a forum with a FAQ section.

▶ www.relaxinggarda.co.uk has regular posts about events, accommodation, shopping, leisure, food and the nightlife around Lake Garda. Their area of interest is health, relaxation and leisure.

Regardless of whether you are still preparing your trip or already on Lake Garda: these addresses will provide you with more information, videos and networks to make your holiday even more enjoyable.

VIDEOS & PODCASTS

▶ www.vistgarda.com/en/video-lake-garda is an excellent four minute Lake Garda promotional video.

▶ www.lake-garda-revealed.com/sailing-video.html this short sailing video gives you an idea of one of the lake's most popular sports. The sailing conditions are excellent and this is the perfect environment to learn the ropes.

▶ www.gardaonbike.com has a great ten minute video of mountain bikers doing the Contrail around northern Lake Garda.

▶ www.xride.it/forum/post74593.html The old Sentiero del Ponale is a beautiful and long route for mountain-bike (see also www.youtube.com/watch?v=KBlmvb-NNqI&feature=related)

▶ www.youtube.com/watch?v=O3vKCYNFqyE The eight minute video shows some of the more than 500 species of flowers and plants. You will also catch glimpses of artwork and sculptures by world famous artists such as Keith Haring.

APPS

▶ Lake Garda iPhone App is an easy to use app for your Lake Garda stay. It includes information on how to get there, highlights, a gallery, weather forecasts and useful phone numbers.

NETWORK

▶ www.igougo.com/travel_guide-l2856-Lake_Garda_tourism.html has travel planning tools and resources to help you create a memorable holiday. There are traveller reviews on local hotels, restaurants and a travel forum where you can ask the advice of fellow travellers.

▶ www.expatsinitaly.com is a site and forum set up to assist future expats to make an easy transition to their new life in Italy. It has lots of information about insurance, property purchase, cost of living and cultural differences as well as a social introduction section.

TRAVEL TIPS

ARRIVAL

People coming from the north, take the route via Austria and the Brenner Pass. Those wanting to save the toll charges, or who prefer to travel more leisurely, can take the old Brenner Pass route. There are two possibilities from Trento: you can drive down into the Sarca valley and approach Lake Garda via Arco and Riva. Or, you drive to the Rovereto South motorway exit and reach Torbole by way of Nago. This route has the advantage that you have a wonderful view of the lake over the last few miles after Nago. Those heading for the southern section of the lake take the motorway exit Affi near Bardolino and Garda.

Holidaymakers travelling through southwest Germany and Switzerland reach Lake Garda along the Gotthard motorway and then the Milan–Venice motorway (exit: Desenzano, Sirmione and Peschiera). You need a vignette if you use the Swiss and Austrian motorways; tolls are levied on motorways in Italy.

The quickest way from Britain by train is with the Eurostar via Paris and then on to Milan. IC and Eurocity trains link other European cities with main Italian destinations. Italy's dense rail network, reasonable ticket prices and reliable train schedules make travelling by rail an excellent way of getting around.

In Rovereto, you can transfer to the public bus service, which will take you directly to the nort shore of Lake Garda. From Verona, take the train to Milan and get off in Peschiera or Desenzano. For further information: www.europeanrail.com, www.euro star.com, www.trainitalia.com and www. raileurope.co.uk

The Italian airline, Alitalia (www.al italia.co.uk) flies out of most international airports. A number of budget operators also serve the area, for example Ryanair (www.ryanair.com), which links London Stansted and Brescia, or easyJet (www.easyjet.com). Numerous carriers operate direct flights from the US (www. alitaliausa.com, www.aa.com, www.united. com, www.delta.com, www.nwa.com). Flying time varies from around 11 hours (US West Coast) to 8 hours (East Coast). There are international airports in Milan, Turin and Venice, smaller ones in Verona, Bergamo and Brescia. From here take the bus, train or hire a car to reach your final destination.

Holiday-makers can often be collected from railway stations and airports; information under www.rivieradeilimoni.it and Transferservice (tel. 036 52 15 51 www.lake gardatransfer.com).

RESPONSIBLE TRAVEL

It doesn't take a lot to be environmentally friendly whilst travelling. Don't just think about your carbon footprint whilst flying to and from your holiday destination but also about how you can protect nature and culture abroad. As a tourist it is especially important to respect nature, look out for local products, cycle instead of driving, save water and much more. If you would like to find out more about eco-tourism please visit: www.ecotourism.org

From arrival to weather

Holiday from start to finish: the most important addresses and information for your Lake Garda trip

BUSES

It cannot be repeated enough: leave your car in the hotel carpark and use public transport! The roads around the lake are chronically jammed. The bus trip from Riva to Limone does not even cost 2 euros – parking in Limone costs 1 euro an hour. Bus timetables can be obtained from all tourist offices and the buses are fairly punctual – traffic permitting. Tickets *(biglietti)* have to be bought before the start of the journey; in the larger villages from the ticket office at the bus station or else from tobacconists. You can also buy one on the bus – but you will have to pay almost double.

CAMPING

Not all shores around Lake Garda are equally suitable for camping; there is too little space in the north due to the sheer rock faces. Most camp sites are in the south, especially in Valtenesi between Desenzano and Salò, and most are of a good standard. The price per night is usually around 13 euros for the site, 8 euros for each adult and 6 euros for each child. See also information on individual villages.

CAR HIRE

There are car-rental firms *(autono-leggio)* – both international and local companies –

MARKETS & MARKET DAYS

Shopping at weekly markets in Italy is a ritual. Not only tourists but the locals also wander from stand to stand. There are, however, lots of poor quality goods imported from Asia but somewhere you will find that stand with salad servers made of olive wood, that vendor of practical kitchenware and, of course, the stand with handbags – 'real leather, *signora*, honestly', belts and jeans, beach towels and tablecloths. Just be careful not to fall for the fake brand-name clothes and bags. Trading with these is illegal – and that applies to whoever buys them as well. Parking places by the way are virtually non-existent on market days. *Mon:* Colombare di Sirmione, Cisano, Moniga del Garda, Peschiera, Torri del Benaco; *Tue:* Castelletto di Brenzone,

Desenzano, Limone (1st and 3rd Tue in the month), Tignale, Torbole (2nd and 4th Tue in the month, but only April–Sept); *Wed:* Arco (1st Wed May–Sept and also 3rd Wed in the month), Lazise, Riva del Garda (2nd Wed June–Sept and also 4th Wed in the month), San Felice del Benaco; *Thu:* Bardolino, Toscolano-Maderno; *Fri:* Garda, Manerba del Garda; *Sat:* Brescia, Malcesine, Salò. Antique markets: *Wed evening:* Torri del Benaco; *1st Thu in the month (May–Oct):* Caprino Veronese; *1st Fri evening in the month (only July/Aug):* Brenzone; *3rd Sat in the month:* Arco, Verona (on Piazza San Zeno); *1st Sun in the month:* Desenzano, Peschiera del Garda; *3rd Sun in the month:* Lonato, Bardolino, Mantua

in many towns around the lake. It is recommended that you book in advance for the high season.

CLIMATE, WHEN TO GO

Lake Garda can be visited at any time of the year. In winter, the temperature seldom dips below freezing point. Only a few hotels are open but this is when the west shore, in particular, displays its *fin-de-siècle* charm. When there is in the mountains and fog lies on the cold and damp Po plain, you may still be able to go for a walk in the sun on Lake Garda. Spring is perhaps the best time to visit Lake Garda: the mild climate is particularly suitable for hiking, the hotel prices are still moderate (except at Easter) and you can easily find somewhere to stay.

In summer it can get pretty hot although the wind off the lake makes the temperature more bearable. The one drawback is that it would appear that everyone in northern Italy wants to spend their holidays here. Weekends in August is bumper-to-bumper time: mile-long traffic jams with stop-and-go on the roads and body contact on the beaches.

Autumn is perfect for hiking. Weeks of stable weather are not unusual and from the top of Monte Baldo you can see from the glaciers to Verona.

CUSTOMS

Travellers from other EU countries are no longer subject to custom checks. EU citizens may bring the following items into Italy (for personal use only): max. 90 L of wine, 10 L of spirits, 800 cigarettes. Duty-free for non-EU citizens are: 50 g perfume, 2 L of wine, 1 L of spirits and 200 cigarettes. US and Canadian customs authorities have details of respective limits for goods brought back from abroad.

When flying into Italy, non-EU citizens require an onward or return ticket.

DRIVING

The maximum speed in built-up areas is 50 km/h (30 mph), on main roads 90 km/h (55 mph), on dual carriageways 110 km/h (66 mph) and 130 km/h (80 mph), on motorways 150 km/h (90 mph). It is mandatory to drive with dipped headlights outside of built-up areas during the day; this applies to motorbike and moped riders everywhere. The blood alcohol limit is 0.5. There must be an emergency jacket for each passenger in the car – inside the car, not in the boot! Italy has recently cracked down on traffic offenders and there are very strict rules to be observed: alcohol is absolutely prohibited under the age of 21 and during the first three years of someone possessing a driving licence. Those who have just passed their test are not allowed to drive faster than 90 km/h on main roads or 100 km/h on motorways. Anyone cycling after dark must wear a high-visibility jacket; children under 14 must wear a cycle helmet, to mention just a few regulations.

Charges are almost always levied when parking in a town and the police hand out tickets with great enthusiasm. With the exception of those located on motorways, most petrol stations close for lunch and on Sundays, although many do have credit card-operated pumps. Breakdown service: toll-free number: *tel. 80 31 16.*

EMBASSIES & CONSULATES

BRITISH CONSULATE GENERAL
Via S. Paolo 7 | Milan | tel. 02 72 30 01 | www.britain.it

US CONSULATE GENERAL
Via Principe Amedeo 2/10 | Milan | tel. 02 29 03 51 | milan.usconsulate.gov

EMBASSY OF CANADA
Via Zara 30 | Rome | tel. 06 854 44 39 37 | www.canada.it

EMERGENCY SERVICES

General emergencies *tel. 112*; police *tel. 113*; fire brigade *tel. 115*; forest fires *tel. 1515*

ENTRANCE FEES

In many museums children under 12 and those over 60 have free entry. Smaller institutions are not expensive but at the major tourist attractions such as Vittoriale and the Giardino Botanico in Gardone, the Cascata del Varone in Riva the Grotte di Catullo in Sirmione expect to pay between 5 and 12 euros.

You can save money with the *Promotion Card*, which entitles you to reductions in museums and leisure parks, such as Vittoriale, Parco Natura Viva, the Arena in Verona, the Hruska Botanic Garden, Gardaland and Caneva-World. Reductions are also given on boat trips and the cable-car in Malcesine. Available in hotels.

FERRIES

● The ferries Maderno–Torri del Benaco (approx. every hour during the day) and Limone–Malcesine (10 times a day) save you driving half way round half the lake. During the peak season a car ferry also

WEATHER IN RIVA

	Jan	Feb	March	April	May	June	July	Aug	Sept	Oct	Nov	Dec
Daytime temperatures in °C/°F												
	5/41	7/45	7/45	17/63	20/68	24/75	27/81	26/79	22/72	16/61	11/52	6/43
Night time temperatures in °C/°F												
	1/34	1/34	4/39	9/48	13/55	17/63	19/66	18/64	15/59	10/50	5/41	2/36
Sunshine hours/day												
	3	4	5	5	6	7	8	7	6	6	3	3
Precipitation days/month												
	5	5	7	9	11	10	8	8	7	8	8	6
Water temperature in °C/°F												
	8/46	6/43	8/46	10/50	13/55	18/64	20/68	21/70	19/66	16/61	12/54	10/50

operates between Riva–Desenzano and back, only stopping at a few places on the way. Passenger ferries between Desenzano and Riva stop at almost all places en route. In the summer season, evening cruises are also held. Timetables available from the tourist information offices and where the boats come in – where you can also buy tickets which must be bought in advance. *www.navigazionelaghi.it*

HEALTH

The least complicated method: in case of illness, pay for your doctor and medicine on the spot and present your bills to the health service when you return home for problem-free reimbursement. The new European Health Insurance Card (EHC) is also accepted.

IMMIGRATION

Visas are not required for EU citizens; citizens of the US or Canada require a visa only if staying for longer than three months. A valid identity card or passport is sufficient to allow entry to Italy.

INFORMATION

ITALIAN GOVERNMENT TOURIST BOARD ENIT

In the UK: *1, Princes Sreet, W1B 2AY London, tel. 020-73 99 35 2;* in the US: *630, Fifth Avenue – Suite 1565, New York, NY, 10111, tel. 212-245 48 22;* in Canada: *175 Bloor Street East – Suite 907, South Tower, M4W 3R8 Toronto, tel. 416-925 48 82.*

INTERNET CAFÉS & WI-FI

You are most likely to find Wi-Fi in large hotels, some motorway restaurants (always advertised well in advance with the Wi-Fi sign) and airports.

In many public squares and streets in towns at the northern end of Lake Garda (Riva, Torbole, Nago and to a certain extent in Malcesine) Wi-Fi is available free of charge. You can surf for a few minutes without registering and then charges are made, either as a text message for those using the Italian mobile phone network or at the reception desk in participating hotels. The one-off registration fee costs 1 euro.

MONEY & CREDIT CARDS

Cash dispenser are available everywhere and the usual credit cards are accepted at petrol stations, virtually all hotels, most restaurants and in many shops.

CURRENCY CONVERTER

£	€	€	£
1	1.10	1	0.90
3	3.30	3	2.70
5	5.50	5	4.50
13	14.30	13	11.70
40	44	40	36
75	82.50	75	67.50
120	132	120	108
250	275	250	225
500	550	500	450

$	€	€	$
1	0.70	1	1.40
3	2.10	3	4.20
5	3.50	5	7
13	9.10	13	18.20
40	28	40	56
75	52.50	75	105
120	84	120	168
250	175	250	350
500	350	500	700

For current exchange rates see www.xe.com

NEWSPAPERS

English-language newspapers and magazines are available at many kiosks. You might get European editions of *The Guardian* and *Financial Times* as well as an italian edition of the *International Herald Tribune* or *USA Today*.

OPENING HOURS

Opening hours are not uniformly regulated in Italy but shops are usually open Mon–Sat 9am–12.30pm and 3.30pm–7.30pm; larger supermarkets usually have no lunch break. In many towns the shops in the pedestrian precincts are open until 10pm. Most grocery stores are also open on Sunday morning.

PHONE & MOBILE PHONE

The country code for Italy is 0039. It is necessary to dial the 0 at the beginning of each fixed-line connection – both from abroad and when making local calls. Mobile telephone numbers (often 338 or 339) are always dialled without 0. Country codes from Italy are 0044 (UK), 001 (US and Canada), 00353 (Ireland), 0061 (Australia), 0064 (New Zealand) and 0027 (South Africa). 170 or 172 followed by the country code will connect you to an operator in your home country and allows you to make international collect calls. Telephone cards can be purchased in most *tabacchi* shops.

Most British mobile phones work without a problem in Italy. You can save roaming charges by choosing the most economical network. You can avoid the fees for incoming calls by using a prepaid card from the country you are visiting. Prepaid cards, such as those from GlobalSim *(www.globalsim.net)*, are expensive but save roaming charges. Texting is always cheap.

Your mailbox can cause high costs: turn it off before you leave home!

BUDGETING

Coffee	1,50–3 euros *for a cappuccino*
Snack	from 3 euros *for a filled panino*
Wine	from 3,50 euros *for ¼ litre*
Olive oil	from 5 euros *for 1 litre olio extravergine*
Fuel	approx. 1,30 euros *for 1 litre Super Euro 95*
Cable-car	18 euros *for return trip up and down Monte Baldo*

POST

Stamps *(francobolli)* are available from post offices, tobacconists *(tabacchi)* but hardly ever where you buy postcards.

PRICES

If you want to enjoy your cappuccino with a view of the lake, be prepared to pay 2.50 or 3 euros instead of the usual 1.50. An aperitif costs from 2.50 euros. If you want to eat more than a pizza (about 6.50 euros) and order in true Italian style: *antipasti*, pasta, main course, wine and dessert you must count on at least 30 – 40 euros per person. It will be hard to find a double room for less than 60 euros.

TIPPING

Five to ten per cent is usual. In restaurants and bars you wait until you are given your change and then leave the tip on the little tray with the bill.

USEFUL PHRASES ITALIAN

PRONUNCIATION

c, cc	before e or i like ch in "church", e.g. ciabatta, otherwise like k
ch, cch	like k, e.g. pacchi, che
g, gg	before e or i like j in "just", e.g. gente, otherwise like g in "get"
gl	like "lli" in "million", e.g. figlio
gn	as in "cognac", e.g. bagno
sc	before e or i like sh, e.g. uscita
sch	like sk in "skill", e.g. Ischia
z	at the beginning of a word like dz in "adze", otherwise like ts

An accent on an Italian word shows that the stress is on the last syllable.
In other cases we have shown which syllable is stressed by placing a dot below
the relevant vowel.

IN BRIEF

Yes/No/Maybe	Sì/No/Forse
Please/Thank you	Per favore/Grazie
Excuse me, please!	Scusa!/Mi scusi
May I ...?/Pardon?	Posso ...? / Come dice?/Prego?
I would like to .../Have you got ...?	Vorrei .../Avete ...?
How much is ...?	Quanto costa ...?
I (don't) like that	(Non) mi piace
good/bad	buono/cattivo/bene/male
broken/doesn't work	guasto/non funziona
too much/much/little/all/nothing	troppo/molto/poco/ tutto/niente
Help!/Attention!/Caution!	aiuto!/attenzione!/prudenza!
ambulance/police/fire brigade	ambulanza/polizia/vigili del fuoco
Prohibition/forbidden/danger/dangerous	divieto/vietato/pericolo/pericoloso
May I take a photo here/of you?	Posso fotografar La?

GREETINGS, FAREWELL

Good morning!/afternoon!/ evening!/night!	Buon giorno!/Buon giorno!/ Buona sera!/Buona notte!
Hello! / Goodbye!/See you	Ciao!/Salve! / Arrivederci!/Ciao!
My name is ...	Mi chiamo ...
What's your name?	Come si chiama?/Come ti chiami
I'm from ...	Vengo da ...

Parli italiano?

"Do you speak Italian?" This guide will help you to say the basic words and phrases in Italian.

DATE & TIME

Monday/Tuesday/Wednesday	lunedì/martedì/mercoledì
Thursday/Friday/Saturday	giovedì/venerdì/sabato
Sunday/holiday/ working day	domenica/(giorno) festivo/ (giorno) feriale
today/tomorrow/yesterday	oggi/domani/ieri
hour/minute	ora/minuto
day/night/week/month/year	giorno/notte/settimana/mese/anno
What time is it?	Che ora è? Che ore sono?
It's three o'clock/It's half past three	Sono le tre/Sono le tre e mezza
a quarter to four	le quattro meno un quarto/ un quarto alle quattro

TRAVEL

open/closed	aperto/chiuso
entrance/exit	entrata/uscita
departure/arrival	partenza/arrivo
toilets/ladies/gentlemen	bagno/toilette/signore/signori
(no) drinking water	acqua (non) potabile
Where is ...?/Where are ...?	Dov'è ...?/Dove sono ...?
left/right/straight ahead/back	sinistra/destra/dritto/indietro
close/far	vicino/lontano
bus/tram	bus/tram
taxi/cab	taxi/tassì
bus stop/cab stand	fermata/posteggio taxi
parking lot/parking garage	parcheggio/parcheggio coperto
street map/map	pianta/mappa
train station/harbour	stazione/porto
airport	aeroporto
schedule/ticket	orario/biglietto
supplement	supplemento
single/return	solo andata/andata e ritorno
train/track	treno/binario
platform	banchina/binario
I would like to rent ...	Vorrei noleggiare ...
a car/a bicycle	una macchina/una bicicletta
a boat	una barca
petrol/gas station	distributore/stazione di servizio
petrol/gas / diesel	benzina/diesel/gasolio
breakdown/repair shop	guasto/officina

FOOD & DRINK

Could you please book a table for tonight for four?	Vorrei prenotare per stasera un tavolo per quattro?
on the terrace/by the window	sulla terrazza/ vicino alla finestra
The menu, please/	La carta/il menù, per favore
Could I please have ...?	Potrei avere ...?
bottle/carafe/glass	bottiglia/caraffa/bicchiere
knife/fork/spoon/salt/pepper	coltello/forchetta/cucchiaio/sale/pepe
sugar/vinegar/oil/milk/cream/lemon	zucchero/aceto/olio/latte/panna/limone
cold/too salty/not cooked	freddo/troppo salato/non cotto
with/without ice/sparkling	con/senza ghiaccio/gas
vegetarian/allergy	vegetariano/vegetariana/allergia
May I have the bill, please?	Vorrei pagare/Il conto, per favore
bill/tip	conto/mancia

SHOPPING

Where can I find...?	Dove posso trovare ...?
I'd like .../I'm looking for ...	Vorrei .../Cerco ...
Do you put photos onto CD?	Vorrei masterizzare delle foto su CD?
pharmacy/shopping centre/kiosk	farmacia/centro commerciale/edicola
department store/supermarket	grandemagazzino/supermercato
baker/market/grocery	forno/ mercato/negozio alimentare
photographic items/newspaper shop/	articoli per foto/giornalaio
100 grammes/1 kilo	un etto/un chilo
expensive/cheap/price/more/less	caro/economico/prezzo/di più/di meno
organically grown	di agricoltura biologica

ACCOMMODATION

I have booked a room	Ho prenotato una camera
Do you have any ... left?	Avete ancora ...
single room/double room	una (camera) singola/doppia
breakfast/half board/	prima colazione/mezza pensione/
full board (American plan)	pensione completa
at the front/seafront/lakefront	con vista/con vista sul mare/lago
shower/sit-down bath/balcony/terrace	doccia/bagno/balcone/terrazza
key/room card	chiave/scheda magnetica
luggage/suitcase/bag	bagaglio/valigia/borsa

BANKS, MONEY & CREDIT CARDS

bank/ATM/pin code	banca/bancomat/ codice segreto
cash/credit card	in contanti/carta di credito
bill/coin/change	banconota/moneta/il resto

HEALTH

doctor/dentist/paediatrician	medico/dentista/pediatra
hospital/emergency clinic	ospedale/pronto soccorso/guardia medica
fever/pain/inflamed/injured	febbre/dolori/infiammato/ferito
diarrhoea/nausea/sunburn	diarrea/nausea/scottatura solare
plaster/bandage/ointment/cream	cerotto/fasciatura/pomata/crema
pain reliever/tablet/suppository	antidolorifico/compressa/supposta

POST, TELECOMMUNICATIONS & MEDIA

stamp/letter/postcard	francobollo/lettera/cartolina
I need a landline phone card/ I'm looking for a prepaid card for my mobile	Mi serve una scheda telefonica per la rete fissa/Cerco una scheda prepagata per il mio cellulare
Where can I find internet access?	Dove trovo un accesso internet?
dial/connection/engaged	comporre/linea/occupato
socket/adapter/charger	presa/riduttore/caricabatterie
computer/battery/rechargeable battery	computer/batteria/accumulatore
internet address (URL)/e-mail address	indirizzo internet/indirizzo email
internet connection/wifi	collegamento internet/wi-fi
e-mail/file/print	email/file/stampare

LEISURE, SPORTS & BEACH

beach/bathing beach	spiaggia/bagno/stabilimento balneare
sunshade/lounger/cable car/chair lift	ombrellone/sdraio/funivia/seggiovia
(rescue) hut/avalanche	rifugio/valanga

NUMBERS

0	zero	15	quindici
1	uno	16	sedici
2	due	17	diciassette
3	tre	18	diciotto
4	quattro	19	diciannove
5	cinque	20	venti
6	sei	21	ventuno
7	sette	50	cinquanta
8	otto	100	cento
9	nove	200	duecento
10	dieci	1000	mille
11	undici	2000	duemila
12	dodici	10000	diecimila
13	tredici	½	un mezzo
14	quattordici	¼	un quarto

NOTES

MARCO POLO TRAVEL GUIDES

ALGARVE
AMSTERDAM
ANDALUCÍA
ATHENS
AUSTRALIA
AUSTRIA
BALI
 LOMBOK,
 GILI ISLANDS
BANGKOK
BARCELONA
BERLIN
BRAZIL
BRUGES, GHENT &
 ANTWERP
BRUSSELS
BUDAPEST
BULGARIA
CALIFORNIA
CAMBODIA
CANADA EAST
CANADA WEST
 ROCKIES
CAPE TOWN
 WINE LANDS,
 GARDEN ROUTE
CAPE VERDE
CHANNEL ISLANDS
CHICAGO
 & THE LAKES
CHINA
COLOGNE
COPENHAGEN
CORFU
COSTA BLANCA
 VALENCIA
COSTA BRAVA
 BARCELONA
COSTA DEL SOL
 GRANADA
CRETE
CUBA
CYPRUS
 NORTH AND
 SOUTH
DRESDEN
DUBAI
DUBLIN
DUBROVNIK &
 DALMATIAN COAST

EDINBURGH
EGYPT
EGYPT'S RED
 SEA RESORTS
FINLAND
FLORENCE
FLORIDA
FRENCH ATLANTIC
 COAST
FRENCH RIVIERA
 NICE, CANNES &
 MONACO
FUERTEVENTURA
GRAN CANARIA
GREECE
HAMBURG
HONG KONG
 MACAU
ICELAND
INDIA
INDIA SOUTH
 GOA & KERALA
IRELAND
ISRAEL
ISTANBUL
ITALY
JORDAN
KOS
KRAKOW
LAKE GARDA

LANZAROTE
LAS VEGAS
LISBON
LONDON
LOS ANGELES
MADEIRA
 PORTO SANTO
MADRID
MALLORCA
MALTA
 GOZO
MAURITIUS
MENORCA
MILAN
MONTENEGRO
MOROCCO
MUNICH
NAPLES &
 THE AMALFI COAST
NEW YORK
NEW ZEALAND
NORWAY
OSLO
PARIS
PHUKET
PORTUGAL
PRAGUE

RHODES
ROME
SAN FRANCISCO
SARDINIA
SCOTLAND
SEYCHELLES
SHANGHAI
SICILY
SINGAPORE
SOUTH AFRICA
SRI LANKA
STOCKHOLM
SWITZERLAND
TENERIFE
THAILAND
TURKEY
TURKEY
 SOUTH COAST
TUSCANY
UNITED ARAB
 EMIRATES
USA SOUTHWEST
VENICE
VIENNA
VIETNAM
ZÁKYNTHOS

- PACKED WITH INSIDER TIPS
- BEST WALKS AND TOURS
- FULL-COLOUR PULL-OUT MAP
 AND STREET ATLAS

ROAD ATLAS

The green line ▬▬ indicates the Trips & Tours (p. 96–101)
The blue line ▬▬ indicates the Perfect Route (p. 30–31)

All tours are also marked on the pull-out map

Photo: Harbour in Garda

Exploring Lake Garda

The map on the back cover shows how the area has been sub-divided

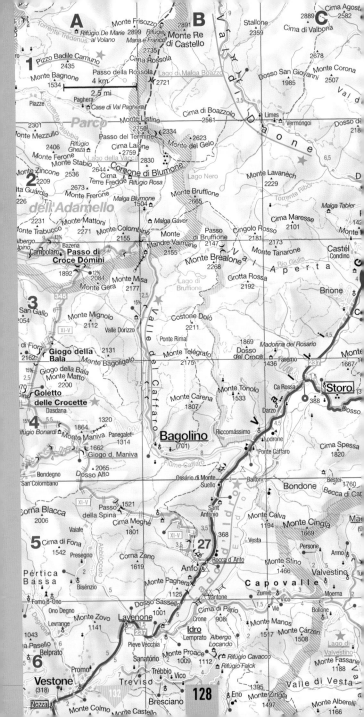

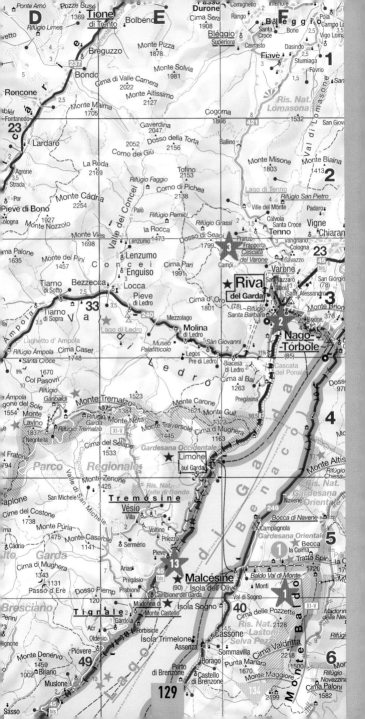

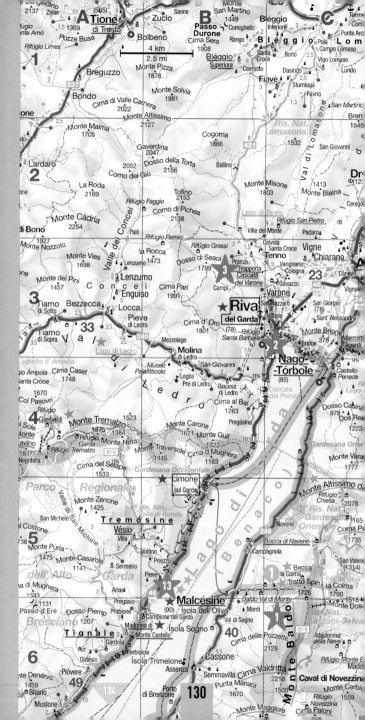

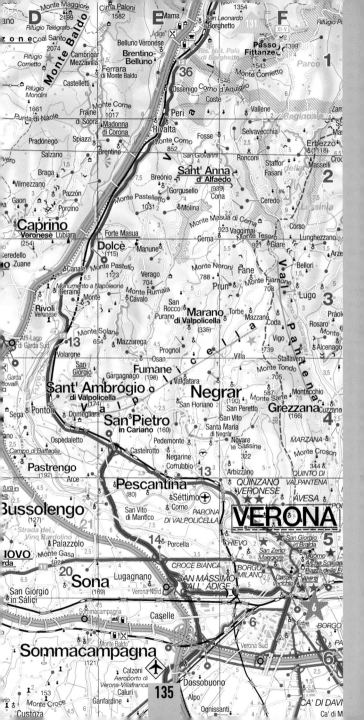

KEY TO ROAD ATLAS

Autobahn · Gebührenpflichtige Anschlussstelle · Gebührenstelle · Anschlussstelle mit Nummer · Rasthaus mit Übernachtung · Raststätte · Kleinraststätte · Tankstelle · Parkplatz mit und ohne WC	Trento	Motorway · Toll junction · Toll station · Junction with number · Motel · Restaurant · Snackbar · Filling-station · Parking place with and without WC
Autobahn in Bau und geplant mit Datum der Verkehrsübergabe	Datum Date	Motorway under construction and projected with completion date
Zweibahnige Straße (4-spurig)		Dual carriageway (4 lanes)
Fernverkehrsstraße · Straßennummern	14 E45	Trunk road · Road numbers
Wichtige Hauptstraße		Important main road
Hauptstraße · Tunnel · Brücke	)=(	Main road · Tunnel · Bridge
Nebenstraßen		Minor roads
Fahrweg · Fußweg		Track · Footpath
Wanderweg (Auswahl)	- - - - - -	Tourist footpath (selection)
Eisenbahn mit Fernverkehr		Main line railway
Zahnradbahn, Standseilbahn	▭▭▭	Rack-railway, funicular
Kabinenschwebebahn · Sessellift	○—○—○ ○+++++○	Aerial cableway · Chair-lift
Autofähre · Personenfähre	● ·········○	Car ferry · Passenger ferry
Schifffahrtslinie		Shipping route
Naturschutzgebiet · Sperrgebiet	////// //////	Nature reserve · Prohibited area
Nationalpark, Naturpark · Wald		National park, natural park · Forest
Straße für Kfz. gesperrt	X X X X X	Road closed to motor vehicles
Straße mit Gebühr	··············	Toll road
Straße mit Wintersperre	‖———‖ XII-II	Road closed in winter
Straße für Wohnanhänger gesperrt bzw. nicht empfehlenswert	🚐 🚐 🚐 🚐	Road closed or not recommended for caravans
Touristenstraße · Pass	Weinstraße ⌃1510	Tourist route · Pass
Schöner Ausblick · Rundblick · Landschaftl bes. schöne Strecke	☆ ☆	Scenic view · Panoramic view · Route with beautiful scenery
Heilbad · Schwimmbad	⚓ ⚓	Spa · Swimming pool
Jugendherberge · Campingplatz	△ X ▲	Youth hostel · Camping site
Golfplatz · Sprungschanze	⚐ /	Golf-course · Ski jump
Kirche im Ort, freistehend · Kapelle	⚑ ⚐	Church · Chapel
Kloster · Klosterruine	⚑ ⚐	Monastery · Monastery ruin
Synagoge · Moschee	☆ ☪	Synagogue · Mosque
Schloss, Burg · Schloss-, Burgruine	⚑ ⚑	Palace, castle · Ruin
Turm · Funk-, Fernsehturm	⌶ ⌶	Tower · Radio-, TV-tower
Leuchtturm · Kraftwerk	⌶ /	Lighthouse · Power station
Wasserfall · Schleuse	⟿ ✝	Waterfall · Lock
Bauwerk · Marktplatz, Areal	□	Important building · Market place, area
Ausgrabungs- u. Ruinenstätte · Bergwerk	∴ ⚒	Arch. excavation, ruins · Mine
Dolmen · Menhir · Nuraghen	π ◻	Dolmen · Menhir · Nuraghe
Hünen-, Hügelgrab · Soldatenfriedhof	☆ ⊞	Cairn · Military cemetery
Hotel, Gasthaus, Berghütte · Höhle	⌂ ∩	Hotel, inn, refuge · Cave

Kultur		**Culture**
Malerisches Ortsbild · Ortshöhe	**WIEN** (171)	Picturesque town · Elevation
Eine Reise wert	★★ **MILANO**	Worth a journey
Lohnt einen Umweg	★ <u>TEMPLIN</u>	Worth a detour
Sehenswert	<u>Andermatt</u>	Worth seeing

Landschaft		**Landscape**
Eine Reise wert	★★ **Las Cañadas**	Worth a journey
Lohnt einen Umweg	★ <u>Texel</u>	Worth a detour
Sehenswert	<u>Dikti</u>	Worth seeing

Ausflüge & Touren		**Excursions & tours**
Perfekte Route		**Perfect route**
MARCO POLO Highlight	★1	**MARCO POLO Highlight**

INDEX

This index lists all sights, museums and places, plus the names of important people featured in this guide. Numbers in bold indicate a main entry.

Affi 17
Albisano 5, **69**
Arco 4, 17, 29, 38, **99**, 102, 103, 104, 107, 110, 111, 114, 115
Assenza 40, 104
Bagnolo di Serniga 94
Bardolino U2, 4, 6, 7, 11, 15, 28, 30, 50, **51**, 60, 110, 111, 115
Bogliaco **86**, 87, 104, 105, 111
Borago 40
Borghetto di Valeggio sul Mincio 63
Brenzone 16, **40**, 104, 115
Bussolengo 54
Campi 46
Campione 31, **88**
Canale di Tenno 46
Caneva-World **108**, 117
Caprino Veronese 115
Carzago di Calvagese della Riviera 104
Cascata del Varone U2, 8, **45**, 117
Cassone 40
Castelletto 40, 110, 115
Castelnuovo 104
Cavaion Veronese 109
Cima delle Pozzette 97
Cima Valdritta 97
Cime di Ventrar 98
Cimitero Militare Tedesco 23
Cisano 29, 52, 55, 104, 115
Colà di Lazise 63, 64
Colombare 78, 79, 115
Costabella 40
Costermano 110
Custoza 16
Desenzano 5, 6, 11, 20, 28, 30, **70**, 79, 104, 114, 115, 118
Dro 17
Eremo di Rocca 59
Eremo Santi Benigno e Caro 40
Fasano 84
Fasse sul Lago 36
Franciacorta Outlet Village 93
Funivia Monte Baldo U2, **40**, 96, 104, 117
Garda 6, 7, 9, 11, 30, 50, 56, 60, 115, 126
Gardacqua 9, **59**
Gardaland 22, 23, 51, 108, **109**, 117
Gardesana Occidentale **20**, 21, 86, 87, 88
Gardone Riviera 4, 9, 11, 20, 31, 80, **81**, 110, 113, 117

Gargnano 5, 11, 27, 29, 31, 80, **86**, 88, 104, 105
Isola del Garda 20, **60**, 91
Isola San Biagio 21, 93
Isola Trimelone 21
Jungle Adventure Park 5, **109**
Lago di Cavedine 99
Lago d'Idro 89
Lago di Ledro **45**, 108
Lago di Lonato 74
Lago di Tenno 45, **46**
Lago di Toblino 96, **99**
Lago di Valvestino 4, **89**
Lazise 8, 30, 50, **61**, 104, 108, 115
Ledro 111
Liano 87
Lido delle Bionde 6, **78**
Lido di Lonato 74
Lido di Padenghe 74
Lido di Ronchi 106
Lido Grotte di Catullo 78
Limone 29, 31, **32**, 38, 103, 104, 110, 111, 115, 117
Linfano 46
Lonato 115
Loncrino 68
Lugana di Sirmione 78
Maderno **85**
Madonna di Montecastello 90
Magasa 89
Magugnano 40
Malcesine 4, 7, 14, 16, 30, 32, **36**, 38, 96, 104, 105, 110, 111, 115, 117, 118
Manerba 93, **94**, 115
Marmitte dei Giganti 46, **48**
Marocche 99
Molina di Ledro 45, 108
Moniga 93
Moniga del Garda 16, 17, 115
Monte Baldo U2, 5, 7, 12, 14, 16, 20, 22, 25, 30, 39, 40, 60, **96**, 102, 104, 113, 116
Monte Brione 49
Montecroce 73
Nago 6, 46, 47, **49**, 114, 118
Navene 38
Novezza 104
Orto Botanico di Monte Baldo 60
Pacengo 106
Palvicio 17
Panzano 39
Parco Alto Garda 19, 20, **107**
Parco Fontanella **87**, 106
Parco Giardino Sigurtà **64**, 109
Parco Natura Viva **109**, 117

Parco Termale del Garda 9
Pastrengo 108
Peschiera 16, 28, 30, **64**, 104, 114, 115
Pieve di Ledro 45
Pieve (Tremosine) 31, **90**
Pieve Vecchia 89, 93
Porto di Brenzone 40
Porto Portese 95
Porto San Felice 93
Prà Alpesina 41
Prabi 107
Prabione 107
Prada 40, 104
Puegnago 95, 104
Punta Cornicello 54, 106
Punta San Vigilio U2, **60**, 61
Riovalli 109
Riva 9, 12, 15, 17, 28, 29, 30, 32, 38, **41**, 99, 102, 103, 104, 105, 106, 110, 111, 114, 115, 117, 118
Rodengo Saiano 93
Rovereto 99, **101**, 114
Salò 6, 8, 13, 14, 20, 27, 28, 31, 80, **90**, 92, 104, 115
San Felice del Benaco 17, 74, **95**, 115
San Martino 46
San Martino della Battaglia 75
San Michele 85
Santa Maria di Lugana 106
San Zeno di Montagna 5, 22, **60**
Sarca valley **99**, 104, 114
Sentiero della Pace 22
Sentiero del Ponale 7, 113
Sentiero del Salt 46
Sirmione U2, 6, 7, 9, 18, 28, 30, 70, **76**, 79, 117
Solferino 70, 75
Spiaggia Comunale Desenzano 74
Spiaggia della Rocca 93
Spiaggia del Tifù 36
Spiaggia Parco Fontanella 106
Spiaggia Rimbalzello 84
Spiaggia Sabbioni U2, 106
Splish Splash 17
Strada dei Vini 93
Strada del Vino 7, 13, 26, **56**
Tempesta 4, 48
Tenno 46
Tignale 22, 115
Torbole 4, 8, 9, 29, 30, 32, 38, **46**, 102, 104, 108, 111, 114, 115, 118

Torri del Benaco 7, 30, 50, **67**, 104, 110, 111, 115, 117
Toscolano-Maderno 7, 15, 20, 31, 67, **85**, 104, 115, 117
Tremosine 5, 20, 31, **90**, 102

Trento 15, 99, **100**
Vajo dell'Orsa 17
Valeggio sul Mincio 17, **63**, 109
Valle delle Cartiere 31
Valtenesi 74, 93, 115

Verona U2, 8, 12, 13, 15, 30, **65**, 111, 114, 115, 117
Vesio 104
Via Santa Lucia 9, **47**
Villa 86, 87, 88
Volta Mantovana 16

WRITE TO US

e-mail: info@marcopologuides.co.uk

Did you have a great holiday?
Is there something on your mind?
Whatever it is, let us know!
Whether you want to praise, alert us to errors or give us a personal tip – MARCO POLO would be pleased to hear from you.
We do everything we can to provide the very latest information for your trip.

Nevertheless, despite all of our authors' thorough research, errors can creep in. MARCO POLO does not accept any liability for this. Please contact us by e-mail or post.

MARCO POLO Travel Publishing Ltd
Pinewood, Chineham Business Park
Crockford Lane, Chineham
Basingstoke, Hampshire RG24 8AL
United Kingdom

PICTURE CREDITS

Cover photograph: M. Riehle
Photos: W. Dieterich (28/29, 91); Divemaster Vivi! (17 bottom); DuMont Bildarchiv: Bernhart (front flap, left, 2 centre top, 7, 27, 30 right, 111, 114 top), Krewitt (110), Mosler (14, 55, 89, 115); ©fotolia.com: eric epoudry (16 centre), rcaucino (16 top); Huber: Friedel (106/107), Huber (3 bottom, 10/11, 64, 86, 96/97), Olimpio (56/57), Potschka (78); Laif: Blickle (83), Bungert (front flap, right), Galli (75), Gerber (18/19), Heidorn (5, 102/103), Zahn (26 right); Look: Martini (90), Pompe (2 centre bottom, 6, 32/33, 82); mauritius images: CuboImages (2 top, 4, 21, 23, 49, 108), FreshFood (24/25); Outdoorplanet: Daniel Schuchter (17 top); M. Riehle (10); O. Stadler (3 centre, 34, 37, 42, 52, 69, 72, 80/81, 85, 98, 114 bottom, 126/127); T. Stankiewicz (2 bottom, 3 top, 12/13, 28, 29, 30 left, 39, 41, 43, 44, 47, 50/51, 58, 61, 70/71, 76/77, 92, 95, 101, 105); M. Thomas (62, 66, 110/111); Vacanselect Reisen GmbH (16 bottom); vario images: imagebroker (8), McPHOTO (20), Westend61 (9, 26 left)

1st Edition 2012

Worldwide Distribution: Marco Polo Travel Publishing Ltd, Pinewood, Chineham Business Park, Crockford Lane, Basingstoke, Hampshire RG24 8AL, United Kingdom. Email: sales@marcopolouk.com
© MAIRDUMONT GmbH & Co. KG, Ostfildern
Chief editor: Marion Zorn
Author: Barbara Schaefer
Editor: Nikolai Michaelis
Programme supervision: Ann-Katrin Kutzner, Nikolai Michaelis, Silwen Randebrock
Picture editor: Barbara Schmid, Gabriele Forst
What's hot: wunder media, München
Cartography road atlas: © MAIRDUMONT, Ostfildern; Cartography pull-out map: © MAIRDUMONT, Ostfildern
Design: milchhof:atelier, Berlin
Front cover, pull-out map cover, page 1: factor product munich
Translated from German by Christopher Wynne; editor of the English edition: Christopher Wynne
Phrase book in cooperation with Ernst Klett Sprachen GmbH, Stuttgart, Editorial by Pons Wörterbücher

DOS & DON'TS

A few things you should bear in mind

GO EVERYWHERE BY CAR

A quick trip to Limone, an afternoon in Malcesine, a swim in Sirmione – but are you sure you want to go by car and leave your (usually free) hotel parking space? Take the boat for a change! You won't get stuck in a traffic jam and won't have to look for an expensive parking place.

VISIT A CHURCH WEARING SPAGHETTI STRAPS

As a rule, the Italians dress fashionably and elegantly. Where tourists drag themselves through the narrow streets of Old Towns in shorts, shirts and sandals, the fashionable Italian woman even wears high heels in difficult terrain (cobblestones). Sitting down at a café table in shorts is really a faux pas. Even worse are men and women who visit churches in inappropriate dress. Cover your shoulders with a blouse or shawl.

ORDER IN ENGLISH

Of course, most Lake Garda waiters will understand you when you order 'a beer'. But, how about learning a handful of Italian words? Drawing the waiter's attention with a *scusi* – excuse me – is almost certain to lead to success.

TRAVEL FROM LAZISE TO PESCHIERA ON A SATURDAY AFTERNOON

The road passes the major leisure parks and when the masses flood out of these the roads become hopelessly jammed.

Just as important: if you want to visit one of these parks, don't do it at the weekend. You will simply be pushed through – especially in August.

FERRAGOSTO ON LAGO DI GARDA

If at all possible, do not travel to Lake Garda around 15 August! That is when all of Italy is on holiday and the traffic comes to a standstill. It is usually just as packed on the beaches around the lake.

BUY FAKE BRAND-NAME ITEMS

Beware of fake brand-name clothing and copies of designer bags. High fines are levied on such transactions – this applies to purchasing, too – also for foreign tourists.

SMOKING

In Italy there is a non-smoking law. As restaurant and café owners would have to pay a high fine in the case of an infringement, they make sure that the law is adhered to – something that nobody ever really thought possible bearing the Italians regard for regulations in mind. This means: you may not light up while drinking an espresso or between courses.